HERMAN CHARLES BOSMAN

JURIE STEYN'S POST OFFICE

Herman Charles Bosman

JURIE STEYN'S POST OFFICE

HUMAN & ROUSSEAU
Cape Town Johannesburg

FIRST EDITION, FIRST IMPRESSION 1971
SECOND IMPRESSION 1974
THIRD IMPRESSION 1978
FOURTH IMPRESSION 1980
FIFTH IMPRESSION 1982
SECOND, COMPLETELY RESET EDITION
FIRST IMPRESSION 1991

Published in uniform edition in 1991 by
Human & Rousseau (Pty) Ltd
State House, 3-9 Rose Street, Cape Town
Cover design by Patricia Going
Cover illustration: "Dwarsberge" (detail)
by Dan Swart
Set in 11 on 13 pt Zapf Book Light
and printed and bound by
National Book Printers, Goodwood

ISBN 0 7981 2903 4

Contents

Compiler's Foreword

During the final year and a half of his life Herman Charles Bosman appears to have worked as though he intimated the brevity of the time left to him. He was employed as a proof reader on the *Sunday Express.* Among his literary relics were found some two hundred pages of an incomplete novel which bore the stamp of current labour. There was also a substantial accumulation of verse manuscripts from many different writers out of which, apparently, he had been selecting an anthology for a publisher. Notes and lists indicated that he had been putting some thought into the compilation of a second collection of his own Groot Marico Stories to follow *Mafeking Road.*

Simultaneously – and this is what makes the period remarkable – he was producing a substantial addition to the Groot Marico canon, in the form of a series under the rubric "In die Voorkamer" (in English, however) which he contributed to *The Forum* weekly.

"Stories" may be a misleading description of the eighty pieces in this series – if "story" suggests a narrative in which characters appear in order to enact an *event* and their dialogue, if any, is the form of their participation in the event. What takes place week by week in Jurie Steyn's voorkamer, which serves as the Drogevlei post office, is essentially not an event, but a conversation.

By and large it is always the same handful of characters who gather to drink Mevrou Steyn's coffee and talk while they await the arrival of the post office lorry from Bekkersdal bringing their letters and milk cans: the farmers Chris Welman, Gysbert van Tonder (known to be the district's biggest cattle smuggler), At Naudé (who is addicted to newspaper reading and radio listening), young Johnny Coen and Oupa Bekker (the oldest inhabitant of the district), and the schoolmaster, young Meneer Vermaak. The course of the conversation between these men and their host as often as not involves the narration of a story by one of them – as often as not by Oupa Bekker who, though pretty strictly within the confines of his platteland world, has seen a thing or two in his time.

There are two points to be made about any stories that do thus get to be narrated. One is that the tale has to be very very lighthandedly and economically developed, to fit the conversational setting and the brief space allowed (the pieces seldom exceed 1 500 words in length). The other is that almost invariably the story is unfolded against a counterpoint consisting in the other characters' always vivacious contribution to the conversation.

Whether or not an actual story gets told in any individual piece, this effect of counterpoint, the interweaving of two or three themes, or procedures, or points of view (this "casual" meandering from level to level, or seemingly off-handed throwing together of incongruous topics or attitudes) is Bosman's most constant device in the Voorkamer. And his employment of it, while justified in terms of psychological realism (conversations are like that) is, I think, original and very effectively serves the ends of enriched meaning, irony, and straight fun (that is to say, the "straight" fun that can result when speakers are grossly at cross-purposes with one another).

The Voorkamer was meant to be the playful corner of *The Forum*, but Bosman's gifts were essentially bound up with playfulness. It was nearly always by playful means that he communicated his most moving and illuminating utterances. This accounts for the popularity his work has achieved: it has made him easy to read – yet, on another level, where the fullness of his intentions lies, it has made him hard to understand. In England, for example, they don't "dig" this particular kind of subtlety.

The point is that, despite the pressure under which it was produced, the Voorkamer series provided an apt vehicle for some of Bosman's special gifts and concerns – his concern, for example, with different kinds of knowledge and different kinds of innocence, his concern with the pressure of change in the world and its effects both on the aesthetic values in our experience and on conduct, his perpetual, fascinated concern with the desires and susceptibilities that motivate people and make them *more* or *less* "human".

As for gifts, his gifts for satire, joke elaboration and characterisation found ample scope in the off-duty atmosphere of the post office-voorkamer. I believe that Oupa Bekker, a less constant, less "professional" raconteur than Oom Schalk Lourens, but a more particularised and *opaque* character, may well come to take a place in South Africa's literary affection not far below that occupied by the narrator of *Mafeking Road* and *Unto Dust.*

Oupa Bekker, in whom backveld narrowness and the broad wisdom of venerable age are indissolubly compounded, is, more nearly than anyone else, the ambiguous hero of the series: to him, time and again, the last word is given. Young Vermaak, propped to the ears with raw book learning, with which he is only too eager to overawe his collocutors, is the equally ambiguous butt. The side Bosman himself is actually on is, however, just about impossible to determine. This is not because his position is objective, but because it is fluid and paradoxical. We can only say for certain that he is *for* life, for humanity, and for laughter.

Out of the eighty pieces that constituted the Voorkamer series I have selected forty which, I feel, after nineteen years still yield pleasure enough to justify their preservation in book form. Several of these I have submitted to some light "editing" to eliminate marks of haste – such as I believe the author himself would have wished corrected before passing them for the bookshelf.

My selection is to be presented in two volumes – *Jurie Steyn's Post Office* being a seemingly perfect title for the first, while the second will be called *A Bekkersdal Marathon.* It might have been desirable to have retained the order in which the pieces originally appeared; but six of them, embodying linked episodes of the "romance" involving Pauline Gerber (a head-turning girl who sends ripples through the Marico scene after her return from a Young Ladies' Finishing School at the

Cape), young Vermaak and Johnnie Coen, are scattered across the middle of the series. So it has been necessary to rearrange the order for the sake of containing the Pauline Gerber "novella" entire in this first volume.

Three of the Voorkamer pieces, *A Bekkersdal Marathon*, *Birth Certificate* and *Day of Wrath*, have already been published in hard covers, in my miscellaneous selection, *Bosman at his Best* – but their true home is Jurie Steyn's post office, and I have no hesitation about repeating them in this selection.

Lionel Abrahams

The Budget

We were sitting in Jurie Steyn's voorkamer at Drogevlei, waiting for the Government lorry from Bekkersdal, that brought us our letters and empty milk cans. Jurie Steyn's voorkamer had served as the Drogevlei post office for some years, and Jurie Steyn was postmaster. His complaint was that the post office didn't pay. It didn't pay him, he said, to be called away from his lands every time somebody came in for a penny stamp. What was more, Gysbert van Tonder could walk right into his voorkamer whenever he liked, and without knocking. Gysbert was Jurie Steyn's neighbour, and Jurie had naturally not been on friendly terms with him since the time Gysbert van Tonder got a justice of the peace and a land-surveyor and a policeman riding a *skimmel* horse to explain to Jurie Steyn on what side of the vlei the boundary fence ran.

What gave Jurie Steyn some measure of satisfaction, he said, was the fact that his post office couldn't be paying the government either.

"Maybe it will pay better now," At Naudé said. "Now that you can charge more for stamps, I mean."

At Naudé had a wireless, and was therefore always first with the news. Moreover, At Naudé made that remark with a slight sneer.

Now, Jurie Steyn is funny in this way. He doesn't mind what he himself says about his post office. But he doesn't care much for the ill-informed kind of comment that he sometimes gets from people who don't know how exacting a postmaster's duties are. I can still remember some of the things Jurie Steyn said to a stranger who dropped in one day for a half-crown postal order, when Jurie had been busy with the cream separator. The stranger spoke of the buttermilk smudges on the postal order, which made the ink run in a blue splotch when he tried to fill it in. It was then that Jurie Steyn asked the stranger if he thought Marico buttermilk wasn't good enough for him, and what he thought he would get for half a crown. Jurie Steyn also started coming from behind the counter, so that he could explain better to the stranger what a man could get in the bushveld for considerably less than half a crown. Unfortunately, the stranger couldn't wait to hear. He said that he had left his engine running when he came into the post office.

From that it would appear that he was not such a complete stranger to the ways of the Groot Marico.

With regard to At Naudé's remark now, however, we could see that Jurie Steyn would have preferred to have let it pass. He took out a thick book with black covers and started ticking off lists with a pencil in an important sort of a way. But all the time we could sense the bitterness against At Naudé that was welling up inside him. When the pencil point broke, Jurie Steyn couldn't stand it any more.

"Anyway, At," he said, "even twopence a half ounce is cheaper than getting a Mchopi runner to carry a letter in a long stick with a cleft in the end. But, of course, you wouldn't understand about things like progress."

Jurie Steyn shouldn't have said that. Immediately three or four of us wanted to start talking at the same time.

"Cheaper, maybe," Johnny Coen said, "but not better, or quicker – or – or – *cleaner.*" Johnny Coen almost choked with laughter. He thought he was being very clever.

Meanwhile, Chris Welman was trying to tell a story we had heard from him often before about a letter that was posted at Christmas time in Volksrust and arrived at its destination, Magoeba's Kloof, twenty-eight years later, and on Dingaan's Day.

"If a Native runner took twenty-eight years to get from Volksrust to Magoeba's Kloof," Chris Welman said, "we would have known that he didn't run much. He must at least have stopped once or twice at huts along the way for kaffir beer."

Meanwhile, Oupa Sarel Bekker, who was one of the oldest inhabitants of the Marico and had known Bekkersdal before it was even a properly measured-out farm, started taking part in the conversation. But because Oupa Bekker was slightly deaf, and a bit queer in the head through advancing years, he thought we were saying that Jurie Steyn had been running along the made road, carrying a letter in a cleft stick. Accordingly, Oupa Bekker warned Jurie Steyn to be careful of mambas. The kloof was full of brown mambas at that time of year, Oupa Bekker said.

"All the same, in the days of the Republics you would not get a white man doing a thing like that," Oupa Bekker went on, shaking his head. "Not even in the Republic of Goosen. And not even after the Republic of Goosen's Minister of Finance had lost all the State revenues in an unfortunate game of poker that he had been invited to take part in at the Mafeking Hotel. And there was quite a big surplus, too, that year, which the Minister of Finance kept tucked away in an inside pocket right through the poker game, and which he could still remember having on him when he went into the bar. Although he could never remember what happened to that surplus afterwards. The Minister of Finance never went back to Goosen, of course. He stayed on in Mafeking. When I saw him again he was offering to help carry people's luggage from the Zeederberg coach station to the hotel."

Oupa Bekker was getting ready to say a lot more when Jurie Steyn interrupted him, demanding to know what all that had got to do with his post office.

"I said that even when things were very bad in the old days, you would still never see a white postmaster running in the sun with a letter in a cleft stick," Oupa Bekker explained, adding, "like a Mchopi."

Jurie Steyn's wife did not want any unpleasantness. So she came and sat on the riempies-bench next to Oupa Bekker and made it clear to him, in a friendly sort of way, what the discussion was all about.

"You see, Oupa," Jurie Steyn's wife said finally, after a pause for breath, "that's just what we have been saying. We've been *saying* that in the old days, before they had proper post offices, people used to send letters with Mchopi runners."

"But that's what I've been saying also," Oupa Bekker persisted. "I say, why doesn't Jurie rather go in his mule cart?"

Jurie Steyn's wife gave it up after that. Especially when Jurie Steyn walked over to where Oupa Bekker was sitting.

"You know, Oupa," Jurie said, talking very quietly, "you have been an ouderling for many years, and we all respect you in the Groot Marico. We also respect your grey hairs. But you must not lose that respect through – through talking about things that you don't understand."

Oupa Bekker tightened his grip on his tambotie-wood walking stick.

"Now if you had spoken to me like that in the Republican days, Jurie Steyn," the old man said, in a cracked voice, "in the Republic of Stellaland, for instance—"

"You and your republics, Oupa," Jurie Steyn said, giving up the argument and turning his back to the counter. "Goosen, Stellaland, Lydenburg – I suppose you were also in the Orighstad Republic?"

Oupa Bekker sat up very stiffly on the riempies-bench, then.

"In the Orighstad Republic," he declared, and in his eyes there gleamed for a moment a light as from a great past, "in the Republic of Orighstad I had the honour to be the Minister of Finance."

"Honour," Jurie Steyn repeated, sarcastically, but yet not speaking loud enough for Oupa Bekker to hear. "I wonder how *he* lost the money in the State's *skatkis.* Playing snakes and ladders, I suppose."

All the same, there were those of us who were much interested in Oupa Bekker's statement. Johnny Coen moved his chair closer to Oupa Bekker, then. Even though Orighstad had been only a small republic, and hadn't lasted very long, still there was something about the sound of the words "Minister of Finance" that could not but awaken in us a sense of awe.

"I hope you deposited the State revenues in the Reserve Bank, in a proper manner," At Naudé said, winking at us, but impressed all the same.

"There was no Reserve Bank in those days," Oupa Bekker said, "or any other kind of banks either, in the Republic of

Orighstad. No, I just kept the national treasury in a stocking under my mattress. It was the safest place, of course."

Johnny Coen put the next question.

"What was the most difficult part of being Finance Minister, Oupa?" he asked. "I suppose it was to make the budget balance?"

"Money was the hardest thing," Oupa Bekker said, sighing.

"It still is," Chris Welman interjected. "You don't need to have been a Finance Minister, either, to know that."

"But, of course, it wasn't as bad as today," Oupa Bekker went on. "Being Minister of Finance, I mean. For instance, we didn't need to worry about finding money for education, because there just wasn't any, of course."

Jurie Steyn coughed in a significant kind of way, then, but Oupa Bekker ignored him.

"I don't think," he went on, "that we would have stood for education in the Orighstad Republic. We knew we were better off without it. And then there was no need to spend money on railways and harbours, because there weren't any, either. Or hospitals. We lived a healthy life in those days, except maybe for lions. And if you died from a lion, there wasn't much of you left over that could be *taken* to a hospital. Of course, we had to spend a good bit of money on defence, in those days. Gunpowder and lead, and oil to make the springs of our old sanna's work more smoothly. You see, we were expecting trouble any day from Paul Kruger and the Doppers. But it was hard for me to know how to work out a popular budget, especially as there were only seventeen income-tax payers in the whole of the Republic. I thought of imposing a tax on the President's state coach, even. I found that that suggestion was very popular with the income-tax paying group. But you have no idea how much it annoyed the President.

"I imposed all sorts of taxes afterwards, which nobody would have to pay. These taxes didn't bring in much in the way of money, of course. But they were very popular, all the same. And I can still remember how popular my budget was, the year I put a very heavy tax on opium. I had heard somewhere about an opium tax. Naturally, of course, I did not expect this tax to bring in a penny. But I knew how glad the burghers of the Orighstad Republic would be, each one of them, to think that there was a tax that they escaped."

Oupa Bekker was still talking about the measures he introduced to counteract inflation in the early days of the Republic of Orighstad, when the lorry from Bekkersdal arrived in a cloud of dust. The next few minutes were taken up with a hurried sorting of letters and packages, all of which proceeded to the background noises of clanking milk cans. Oupa Bekker left when the lorry arrived, since he was expecting neither correspondence nor a milk can. The lorry driver and his assistant seated themselves on the riempies-bench which the old man had vacated. Jurie Steyn's wife brought them in coffee.

"You know," Jurie Steyn said to Chris Welman, in between putting sealing wax on a letter he was getting ready for the mailbag. "I often wonder what is going to happen to Oupa Bekker – such an old man and all, and still such a liar. All that Finance Minister rubbish of his. How they ever appointed him an ouderling in the church, I don't know. For one thing, I mean, he couldn't even have been *born,* at the time of the Orighstad Republic." Jurie reflected for a few moments. "Or could he?"

"I don't know," Chris Welman answered truthfully.

A little later the lorry driver and his assistant departed. We heard them putting water in the radiator. Some time afterwards we heard them starting up the engine, noisily, the driver swearing quite a lot to himself.

It was when the lorry had already started to move off that Jurie Steyn remembered about the registered letter on which he had put the seals. He grabbed up the letter and was over the counter in a single bound.

Chris Welman followed him to the door. He watched Jurie Steyn for a considerable distance, streaking along in the sun behind the lorry and shouting and waving the letter in front of him, and jumping over thorn bushes.

"Just like a Mchopi runner," Chris Welman said.

Ghost Trouble

They were having ghost trouble again in the Spelonksdrift area, Chris Welman said to us when we were sitting in Jurie Steyn's post office. The worst kind of ghost trouble, Chris Welman added.

We could guess what that meant.

Everybody knew, of course, that Spelonksdrift was swarming with ghosts, any time after midnight. The ghosts came out of the caves in the Dwarsberge nearby. During the day it was quite all right. Then even the most difficult spectres would go and lie down in the hollowed-out places at the foot of the koppie and try and get some rest. But after dark they would make their way to the drift, dragging chains and carrying on generally. That much we all knew. I mean, there was not even a Mtosa cattleherd so ignorant as willingly to venture near the drift after nightfall.

When it comes to having to do with ghosts, a Mtosa can be almost as educated as a white man.

Again, with regard to ghosts, we could still remember the time when the new schoolteacher, Charlie Rossouw, who was fresh from college, taught the standard five class, in the history lesson, about the Great Trek. He was talking about the Voortrekker leader, Lodewyk Loggenberg, and about the route his party took, and about the Dagboek that Lodewyk Loggenberg kept. The young schoolteacher said that he did not want his class to think of history as just names of persons that they had to remember, but that the Voortrekkers belonged to their own nation, and were people like their own fathers, say, or – if that was too unpleasant a thought – perhaps like their uncles.

Then, drawing on the blackboard with a piece of chalk, Charlie Rossouw explained to the class that Lodewyk Loggenberg had passed through the Groot Marico with his wagons. "Perhaps the trek passed right in front of where this schoolhouse is today," the teacher said. "Maybe Lodewyk Loggenberg's long line of wagons, with voorryers and agterryers and with the Statebybel in the *bok* and with copper moulds from which to make candles six at a time after you had fixed the wick in the middle, properly (I mean, you know the difference now between a form candle and a water candle: we did that last week) – maybe those Voortrekkers passed along right here, and the tracks that their wagon wheels made over the veld were the beginning of what we today call the government road. Think of that. I wonder what Lodewyk Loggenberg wrote in his Dagboek when he went along this way towards Spelonksdrift? What he thought of this part of the country, I mean. That grand old Patriarch. Does anybody here know what a Patriarch is?"

Practically every child in that standard five class put up his or her hand, then. No, they did not know what a Patriarch was. But they did know what Lodewyk Loggenberg wrote in his Dagboek about Spelonksdrift. And they told the schoolmaster. And the schoolmaster, because he was young and fresh from college, laughed in a lighthearted manner at the answers the pupils gave him. It was all the same answer, really. And it was only after Faans Grobler, who was chairman of our school committee, had spoken earnestly to Charlie Rossouw about how serious a thing it was to laugh at a standard five pupil when he gave the right answer, that Charlie Rossouw went to Zeerust on a push-bicycle over a weekend. Charlie Rossouw spent several hours in the public library at Zeerust. When he came back he was a changed man.

After that, he put in even more time than he had done in the Zeerust library in explaining to standard five – which was the top class – that he had not known, until then, that that particular passage about the haunted character of Spelonksdrift appeared in Lodewyk Loggenberg's Dagboek. He had never been taught that at university, Charlie Rossouw said. But it was clear enough now, of course. He had read it in print. It gave him an insight into Lodewyk Loggenberg's mind that he did not have before, he acknowledged. But then, while he was at the teachers' college, he was not able to go into all those details about South African history. He had to study subjects like blackboard work and cardboard modelling and the theory of education and the depth of the Indian Ocean and the Scholastic Philosophers, including Archbishop Anselm and Thomas Aquinas and Peter Lombard and Duns Scotus. And there was also Albertus Magnus, Charlie Rossouw said. So he should not be blamed for not knowing *everything* that Lodewyk Loggenberg wrote in his Dagboek. He had been so busy, night after night, trying to make out what Duns Scotus was trying to get at. But now that he had himself gone into the world a bit, the schoolmaster said, it seemed to him that there was quite a lot in common between Duns Scotus and Lodewyk Loggenberg. In his opinion, they would both of them have got pretty high marks for cardboard modelling.

Francina Smit, who was in standard five, and who was good at arithmetic, said afterwards that Charlie Rossouw made that remark with what she could only describe as a sneer.

All the same, Charlie Rossouw said to his class, even though it was true that Lodewyk Loggenberg *had* written those things about Spelonksdrift in his Dagboek, it would be best if the class kept quiet about it when the inspector came. He was sure that the school inspector would misunderstand an answer like that. He did not believe that the inspector knew Lodewyk Loggenberg's Dagboek very well. He even went so far as to doubt whether the school inspector knew much about Thomas Aquinas.

A little later, when Charlie Rossouw was sacked from the Education Department, we in the Groot Marico were pleased about it. There was just something about Charlie Rossouw that made us feel he was getting too big for his boots. The next thing he would be telling his class was that the earth turns round the sun. Whereas you've only got to lie in the tamboekiegrass on Abjaterskop towards evening and *watch*, and you'll see for yourself that it isn't so. All those astronomers and people like that – where would they be if they once lay on Abjaterskop in the setting sun, and shredded a plug of roll tobacco with a pocket knife, in the setting sun, and looked about them, and thought a little?

Anyway, even though we who were sitting in Jurie Steyn's voorkamer, that also served as the Dwarsberg post office, were not astronomers, or anywhere near, we were nevertheless much impressed by Chris Welman's statement that they were having ghost trouble at Spelonksdrift. When it came to seeing a ghost you didn't need to be an astronomer and to have a telescope: a ghost was something that you could actually see best just with the naked eye.

Now, if the spirits of the dead were content to haunt only the drift after nightfall, then no harm could come to any human being. No human being was ever *there* after nightfall. It was when a pale apparition took to the road, and wandered through the poort to have a look round, that unfortunate incidents occurred.

If you were travelling along the government road at night and you saw a person walking – or riding on horseback, even – and you saw the moon shining through that person, then you would know, of course, that you had met a ghost. If there was no moon, then you would see the stars shining through the ghost. Or you might even see a withaak tree or a piece of road showing through the ghost.

Gysbert van Tonder once encountered an elderly ghost, riding a mule, right in the middle of the poort. And Gysbert van Tonder held long converse with the ghost, whom he took to be an elderly farmer that had come back from a dance at Nietverdiend – coming back so late because he was elderly. It was when Gysbert van Tonder recognised the mule that the elderly farmer was sitting on as old Koffiebek, that had belonged to his grandfather and that had died many years before of grass-belly, that Gysbert van Tonder grew to have doubts. What made him suspicious, Gysbert van Tonder said, was that he had never in his life seen Koffiebek standing so still, with a man sitting on his back, talking. During the whole conversation Koffiebek did not once try to bite a chunk out of his rider's leg. In the same moment Gysbert van Tonder realised that it was because there wasn't much of his rider for Koffiebek to bite.

"What made it all so queer," Gysbert van Tonder said, "was that I had been talking to the elderly farmer on the mule about a new comet that there was in the sky, then. And I had asked him if he thought it meant the end of the world, and he said he hoped not, because there were several things that he wanted to do still. And it didn't strike me that, all the time we were talking about the comet, the old farmer was sitting between me and the comet, and I was seeing the comet through the middle of his left lung. I could see his right lung, too, the way it swelled out when he breathed."

It was getting late, not only in Jurie Steyn's post office, but everywhere in the Marico, and the lorry from Bekkersdal had not yet arrived with our letters and milk cans. They must be having trouble along the road, we said to each other.

And because of the line of conversation that Chris Welman had started, we were glad when Jurie Steyn, on his return from the milking shed, lit the paraffin lamp in the voorkamer before it was properly dark.

Oupa Bekker had been very quiet, most of the evening. Several times he had looked out into the gathering dusk, shaking his head at it. But after Jurie Steyn had lit the oil lamp, Oupa Bekker cheered up a good deal. Then he started telling us about the time when *he* encountered a ghost near Spelonksdrift, in the old days.

"I had lost my way in the dark," Oupa Bekker declared, "and so I thought that that stretch of water was just an ordinary crossing over the Malopo River. I had no idea that it was Spelonksdrift. So I pulled up at the edge of the stream to let my horse drink. Mind you, I should have known that it was Spelonksdrift just through my horse not having been at all thirsty. Indeed, afterwards it struck me that I had never before seen a horse with so little taste for water. All he did was to look slowly about him and shiver."

At Naudé asked Jurie Steyn's wife to turn the paraffin lamp up a bit higher, just about then. He said he was thinking of the lorry driver. The lorry driver would be able to see the light in Jurie Steyn's voorkamer from a long way off, if the lamp was turned up properly, At Naudé explained. It was queer how several of us, at that moment, started feeling concern for the lorry driver. We all seemed to remember, at once, that he was a married man with five children. Jurie Steyn's wife did not have to turn much on the screw to make the lamp burn brighter. We men did it all for her. But then, of course, we Groot Marico men are chivalrous that way.

In the meantime, Oupa Bekker had been drooling on in his old-man way of talking, with the result that when we were back in our seats again we found that we had missed the in-between part of his story. All we heard was the end part. We heard about his dispute with the ghost, that had ended in the ghost letting him have it across the chops with the back of his hand.

"So I went next day to see Dr Angus Stuart," Oupa Bekker continued. "In those days he was the only doctor between here and Rysmierbult. I didn't tell him anything about what had happened at Spelonksdrift. I just showed him my face, with those red marks on it . . . And do you know what? After he had had a good look at those marks through a magnifying glass, the doctor said that they could have been caused only by a ghost hitting me over the jaw with the back of a blue-flame hand."

That story started Johnny Coen off telling us about the time he was walking through the poort, one night, with Dawie Ferreira, who had once been a policeman at Newclare. And while he and Dawie Ferreira were walking through the poort, a Bechuana through whom they could see the Milky Way shining came up to them. In addition to having the Milky Way visible through his spine, the Bechuana was also carrying his head under his arm. But Dawie Ferreira, because he was a former policeman, knew how to deal with that Bechuana, Johnny Coen said. He promptly asked him where his pass was for being on a public road at that time of night. You couldn't see the Bechuana for dust after that, Johnny Coen said. In fact, the dust that the Bechuana with his head under his arm raised on the government road of the Marico seemed to become part of, and to reach beyond, the Milky Way that shone through his milt and was also a road.

The lorry from Bekkersdal arrived very late. The driver looked perturbed.

"We had big-end trouble at Spelonksdrift," the lorry driver said, "and an old farmer riding a mule came up and gave me a lot of sauce. He acted as though he was a ghost, or something. As though I'd take notice of that sort of nonsense. I saw through him, all right. Then he sloshed me one across the jaw. When I tried to land him one back he was gone."

The lorry driver had marks on his cheek that could have been caused by a back-hander from an elderly farmer riding a mule.

White Ant

Jurie Steyn was rubbing vigorously along the side of his counter with a rag soaked in paraffin. He was also saying things which, afterwards, in calmer moments, he would no doubt regret. When his wife came into the voorkamer with a tin of Cooper's dip, Jurie Steyn stopped using that sort of language and contented himself with observations of a general nature about the hardships of life in the Marico.

"All the same, they are very wonderful creatures, those little white ants," the schoolmaster remarked. "Among the books I brought here into the Marico, to read in my spare time, is a book called *The Soul of the White Ant*. Actually, of course, the white ant is not a true ant at all. The right name for the white ant is isoptera –"

Jurie Steyn had another, and shorter, name for the white ant right on the tip of his tongue. And he started saying it, too. Only, he remembered his wife's presence in time, and so he changed the word to something else.

"This isn't the first time the white ants have got in behind your counter," At Naudé announced. "The last lot of stamps you sold me had little holes eaten all round the edges."

"That's just perforations," Jurie Steyn announced. "All postage stamps are that way. Next time you have got a postage stamp in your hand, just look at it carefully, and you'll see. There's a law about it, or something. In the department we talk of those little holes as perforations. It is what makes it possible for us, in the department, to tear stamps off easily, without having to use a scissors. Of course, it's not everybody that knows that."

At Naudé looked as much hurt as surprised.

"You mustn't think I am so ignorant, Jurie," he announced severely. "Mind you, I'm not saying that, perhaps, when this post office was first opened, and you were still new to affairs, and you couldn't be expected to *know* about perforations and things, coming to this job raw, from behind the plough – I'm not saying that you mightn't have cut the stamps loose with a scissors, or a no. 3 pruning shears, even. At the start, mind you. And nobody would have blamed you for it, either. I mean, nobody ever has blamed you. We've all, in fact, admired the way you took to this work. I spoke to Gysbert van Tonder about it, too, more than once. Indeed, we both admired you. We spoke about how you stood behind that counter, with kraal manure in your hair, and all, just like you were Postmaster General. Bold as brass, we said, too."

The subtle flattery in At Naudé's speech served to mollify Jurie Steyn.

"You said all that about me?" he asked. "You did?"

"Yes," At Naudé proceeded smoothly. "And we also admired the neat way you learnt to handle the post-office rubber stamp, Gysbert and I. We said you held on to it like it was a branding iron. And we noticed how you would whistle, too, just before bringing the rubber stamp down on a parcel, and how you would step aside afterwards, quickly, just as though you half expected the parcel to jump up and poke you in the short ribs. To tell you the truth, Jurie, we were *proud* of you."

Jurie Steyn was visibly touched. And so he said that he admitted he had perhaps been a bit arrogant in the way he had spoken to At Naudé about the perforations. The white ants *had* got amongst his postage stamps, Jurie Steyn acknowledged – once. But what they ate you could hardly notice, he said. They just chewed a little around the edges.

But Gysbert van Tonder said that, all the same, that was enough. His youngest daughter was a member of the Sunshine Children's Club of the church magazine in Cape Town, Gysbert said. And his youngest daughter wrote to Aunt Susann, who was the woman editor, to say that it was her birthday. And when Aunt Susann mentioned his youngest daughter's birthday in the Sunshine Club corner of the church magazine, Aunt Susann wrote that she was a little girl staying in the lonely African wilds. *Gramadoelas* was the word that Aunt Susann used, Gysbert van Tonder said. And all just because Aunt Susann had noticed the way that part of the springbok on the stamp on his youngest daughter's letter had been eaten off by white ants, Gysbert van Tonder said.

He added that his daughter had lost all interest in the Sunshine Children's Club, since then. It sounded so uncivilised, the way Aunt Susann wrote about her.

"As though we're living in a grass hut and a string of crocodiles around it, with their teeth showing," Gysbert van Tonder said. "As though it's all still konsessie farms and we haven't made improvements. And it's no use trying to explain to her, either, that she must just feel sorry for Aunt Susann for not knowing any better. You can't explain things like that to a child."

Nevertheless, while we all sympathised with Gysbert van Tonder, we had to concede that it was not in any way Jurie Steyn's fault. We had all had experience of white ants, and we knew that mostly, when you came along with the paraffin and Cooper's dip, it was too late. By the time you saw those little tunnels, which the white ants made by sticking grains of sand together with spit, all the damage had already been done.

The schoolmaster started talking some more about his book dealing with the life of the white ant, then, and he said that it was well known that the termite was the greatest plague of tropic lands. Several of us were able to help the schoolmaster right. As Chris Welman made it clear to him, the Marico was not in the tropics at all. The tropics were quite a long way up. The tropics started beyond Mochudi, even. A land-surveyor had established that much for us, a few years ago, on a coloured map. It was loose talk about wilds and gramadoelas and tropics that gave the Marico a bad name, we said. Maybe we did have white ants here – lots of them, too – but we certainly weren't in the tropics, like some countries we knew, and that we could mention, also, if we wanted to. Maybe what had happened was that the white ants had come down here *from* the tropics, we said. From away down beyond Mochudi and other side Frik Bonthuys's farm, even. *There* was tropics for you, now, we said to the schoolmaster. Why, he should just see Frik Bonthuys's shirt. Frik Bonthuys wore his shirt outside of his trousers, and the back part of it hung down almost on to the ground.

The schoolmaster said that he thought we were perhaps just a little too sensitive about this sort of thing. He himself was interested in the white ant, he explained, mainly from the scientific point of view. The white ant belonged to the insect world, which was really very highly civilised, he said. All the insect world didn't have was haemoglobin. The insect had the same blood in his veins as a white man, the schoolmaster said, except for haemoglobin.

Gysbert van Tonder said that whatever that thing was, it was enough. Gysbert said it quite hastily, too. He said that when once you started making allowances for the white ant, that way, the next thing the white ant would want would be to vote. And *he* wouldn't go into a polling booth alongside of an ant, to vote, Gysbert van Tonder said, even if that ant *was* white.

This conversation was getting us out of our depths. The talk had taken a wrong turning, but we couldn't make out where, exactly. Consequently, we were all pleased when Oupa Bekker spoke, and made things seem sensible again.

"The worst place I ever knew for white ants, in the old days," Oupa Bekker said, "was along the Malopo, just below where it joins the Crocodile River. *There* was white ants for you. I was a transport rider in those days, when all the transport was still by ox-wagon. My partner was Jan Theron. We called him Jan Mankie because of his wooden leg – a back wheel of the ox-wagon having gone over his kneecap one day when he had been drinking mampoer. Anyway, we had camped out beside the Malopo. And the next morning, when we inspanned, Jan Mankie was saying how gay and *light* he felt. He couldn't understand it. He even started thinking that it must be the drink again, that was this time affecting him in quite a new way. We didn't know, of course, that it was because the white ants had hollowed out all of his wooden leg while he had lain asleep.

"And what was still more queer was that the wagon, when he inspanned it, also seemed surprisingly light. It didn't strike us what the reason for that was, either, just then. Maybe we were not in a guessing frame of mind, that morning. But when our trek got through the Paradys Poort, into a stiff wind that was blowing across the vlakte, it all became very clear to us. For the sudden cloud of dust that went up was not just dust from the road. Our wagon and its load of planed Oregon pine were carried away in the finest kind of powder you can imagine, and all that our oxen were left pulling was the trek-chain. And Jan Mankie Theron was standing on one leg. His other trouser leg, that was of a greyish-coloured moleskin, was flapping empty in the wind."

Thus, Oupa Bekker's factual account of a straightforward Marico incident of long ago, presenting the ways and characteristics of the termite in a positive light, restored us to a sense of current realities.

"But what are you supposed to do about white ants, anyway?" Johnny Coen asked after a while. "Cooper's dip helps, of course. But there should be a more permanent way of getting rid of them, I'd imagine."

It was then that we all turned to the schoolmaster, again. What did it say in that book of his about the white ant, we asked him.

Well, there was a chapter in his book on the destruction of termites, the schoolmaster said. At least, there had been a chapter. It was the last chapter in the book. But he had unfortunately left the book lying on his desk in the schoolroom over one weekend. And when he had got back on Monday morning there was a little tunnel running up his desk. And the pages dealing with how to exterminate the white ant had been eaten away.

Home From Finishing School

We knew, from having heard Jurie Steyn's wife talking to her, that Pauline Gerber was out there, alighting from the lorry. We men, sitting in the voorkamer, would have liked to have gone out and bid Pauline welcome home to the Marico. But we were restrained by a feeling of shyness. For, as Gysbert van Tonder said, she had just come back from the finishing school where she had been learning English manners and freehand drawing, and it would not be becoming for us to go and push ourselves forward, there at the lorry, in just our rough farm clothes, and not able to play the piano.

At Naudé, tiptoeing up to the window, did, however, venture to raise a corner of the chintz curtain. We had always known that Pauline Gerber was pretty, of course. And from the low whistle that At Naudé gave now, we were able to gather that concentration on the schedule of studies at the young ladies' academy had not spoilt her looks.

"Well, of all the pie-faced," At Naudé said suddenly, with a pronounced sneer, "the *pie*-faced . . . well, I give up . . . Drivelling old woman, I should say."

At Naudé made further remarks that did not seem to fit in with the meaning of that first whistle. Could it be, we wondered, that on closer inspection of Pauline, the money spent by her father on her higher education would appear to have been the price of so many head of cattle poured down the drain?

Already Oupa Bekker was weighing in with an historically authentic account of the ruin that got visited on the Van der Sandt family through the attendance of some of its junior members at the Volksgimnasium. The Malope Van der Sandts, Oupa Bekker added.

"It's that lorry driver's assistant," At Naudé explained. "He comes and plonks himself down right in front of her, and stands there by the radiator, talking to her as free and easy as you like. So all I can see right now is a bit of the feather on her hat. He's talking, standing on one leg. Anybody would think he's just come out of college, where they teach you flower arrangements and higher –"

"Higher sums," Gysbert van Tonder interjected, remembering something of his own primary school curriculum and attaching to it imagined academic elevations, "and higher spelling and higher recitation and higher –"

"And now he's shifted onto his other leg," At Naudé continued. "And he's still talking . . . Ha, ha, ha. No, that really was funny. Ha, ha, ha. He was changing legs again. And he just leant his one hand – as airy as you please – right on the radiator. Ha, ha, ha. He's lifting both his legs quite a bit off the ground, now, the way he's jumping. You can imagine how hot the radiator must be of a government lorry that's come without a stop, except Post-bag Helbult, all the way from Bekkersdal, uphill."

Thereupon we all said, ha, ha.

In the same moment At Naudé dropped the corner of the chintz curtain quickly and returned to his riempies-chair. A little later two large but nevertheless trim-looking suitcases came in through the half-open door. The lorry driver's assistant came in with them. It was our turn to whistle, then – even though, unlike At Naudé, we had not yet seen Pauline. We whistled because it was the first time we had ever seen the lorry driver's assistant so polite to a passenger. When it came to not being polite to a passenger, we knew that the lorry driver's assistant was a lot worse even than the lorry driver himself. This was easy enough to understand, of course, seeing that the lorry driver's assistant was trying to get promotion, and he had already learnt that the only way to get anywhere in the service was by being insulting enough to passengers.

But when Pauline Gerber came into the voorkamer we could see why the lorry driver's assistant just didn't care then about all the chances of promotion that he was sacrificing through carrying in a passenger's luggage. He could make up for it later on by losing a milk can in a donga, maybe. Or by throwing a lighted cigarette-end among a Mtosa passenger's blankets, perhaps.

The point is that Pauline Gerber wasn't merely pretty. She brought into Jurie Steyn's voorkamer more than just good looks. And more than you could learn at just a finishing school, for that matter. As Gysbert van Tonder said about it afterwards, Pauline Gerber's coming into the voorkamer was like the middle part of a song of which he had forgotten the words but that he could play the tune of with a comb and tissue paper. And Oupa Bekker said – also afterwards – that, far from the middle or any other part of Pauline's entrance being forgotten, it was like something that would be ever remembered. In story and in song, Oupa Bekker added.

Anyway, there it was. The suitcases came in first, with the lorry driver's assistant walking a little behind the handle of one of the suitcases, going a bit gingerly on that side, as though the heated radiator of the lorry hadn't done his palm much good. Then came Pauline Gerber, with Jurie Steyn's wife following in the rear.

"Not there!" Jurie Steyn's wife called out as the lorry driver's assistant made ready to swing the suitcases onto the post-office counter, nearly knocking over the brass scale and the pen-and-ink stand.

"But I can't put them on the floor," the lorry driver's assistant mumbled, dropping the suitcases on the floor, all the same. "Wet cow dung."

The post-office floor had just recently been smeared.

The sound that Jurie Steyn's wife made sounded a lot like a snort.

"Ho," Jurie Steyn's wife said, "and since when isn't cow dung good enough for you, mister? Something seems to have turned your head, all right. Maybe you can tell us what kind of dung is good enough for you? Come on, speak up. Elephant, maybe, or . . . or . . ."

The lorry driver's assistant looked embarrassed.

"Trouble is I burnt myself on that *verdomde* radiator," he announced, studying the inside of his hand. "It's all blisters."

Jurie Steyn's wife sniffed elegantly.

In doing so she inhaled some of the aroma from the newly-smeared floor that was blended – a trifle incongruously, perhaps – with the perfume that Pauline Gerber had bought at the Cape. That much came out in her next remark.

"Something has turned your head, all right," Jurie Steyn's wife said to the lorry driver's assistant, "something that has made you turn up your nose at my floor. The same thing that made you stand there all simpering in front of the lorry, I'm sure. And that's how you got burnt. Now, if my floor isn't good enough for those two suitcases, then what you could do, see, is to sit down on that bench, there, and hold the two suitcases in your lap. Or is there something else, rather, that you would like to hold in your lap? Not that *she'd* object very much, I should imagine."

Later on, when we discussed the matter between ourselves, in private, we said, yes, we did notice how much of the conversation in the post office that afternoon seemed to have taken on something of a low tone. That was what women's influence was on company, we said. The talk in the voorkamer had never got so low, really, we said, in all the time we could recall when there were only men. Or perhaps men and just one woman, Gysbert van Tonder said. And so we said, afterwards, that, yes, it was all right when it was just men, or just men and one woman. But when it was men and there were two women, we said, then the tone of the talk got lowered in a way that we just couldn't understand. That was what we said afterwards, in private, to each other.

Pauline Gerber took no notice of the insinuations made by Jurie Steyn's wife. You could see she had been taught that it was not ladylike to show her annoyance openly. Instead, Pauline stood straight up in the middle of the voorkamer and gazed slowly about her, at the men sitting on the chairs and benches. And a look of disappointment came over her face. It was almost as though there was something about our appearance that was distressing her. But we knew it couldn't be that, of course. We realised that we were not all as handsome as Johnny Coen, for instance, but we knew that as a collection of manly-looking farmers (and not sissies) we could hold our own with any bunch of men that you could pick anywhere from between the Orange River and the Caprivi Strip. Pretty though she was, Pauline Gerber must not start giving herself airs now, we thought.

Then Jurie Steyn spoke. "Can't one of you fat loafers," Jurie Steyn shouted from behind his counter, "get up and give the young lady a seat?"

We all jumped up then, of course. Well, if that was all it was, we knew our manners, all right, even though we hadn't been to any higher ladies' college. In a moment there were half-a-dozen chairs for Pauline Gerber to pick from. And we didn't make an issue of it with Jurie Steyn, either, for what he had said about fat loafers.

Thereupon Pauline Gerber explained, in dark sweet tones, that what worried her was that nobody of her family was there to take her home. There must have been some sort of misunderstanding, she said. It was the first time she had spoken. Her words had an extraordinary effect on Jurie Steyn.

"I'll drive you home in my mule cart," Jurie Steyn said. "My wife can look after the post office while I'm away."

We were all much impressed with the well-bred and modest fashion in which Pauline Gerber accepted Jurie's invitation.

Some time later, however, when Jurie Steyn called out from the front of the post office to say that the mules were inspanned, we wondered if that young ladies' academy in the Cape really had changed Pauline Gerber so very much. It was when Pauline walked out of the front door, with her chin still in the air. And it wasn't what she did so much as the way she did it, that made it look as though she was at heart still very much of a Marico bushveld girl. The way she sort of half lifted her skirts at Jurie Steyn's wife, when she went out.

Young Man In Love

Gysbert van Tonder told us, in Jurie Steyn's voorkamer, that afternoon, that Johnny Coen would be along later. He had seen Johnny Coen, Gysbert said, by the mealie lands, and Johnny Coen was busy scraping some of the worst turf soil off his veldskoens with a pocket-knife that had only the short blade left. Johnny Coen was also making use of various wisps of yellow grass, performing wiping movements along the side of his face. Well, we all knew that if, in the middle of the ploughing season, a man took all that trouble with his personal appearance, it must be that he was thinking of going visiting.

"Of course, it doesn't necessarily mean that he's coming *here*," At Naudé observed. "I mean, if he was busy to make himself *so* smart, well, it might perhaps mean that he was working up the courage to go and see *her*. You know what I mean – Johnny Coen taking all the trouble to get the turf soil off his veldskoens *and* to get the turf soil off his face.

"If he was coming just here to see us, well, he wouldn't care how much black turf there was on his face. All he would be concerned about was that he didn't leave a lot of thick mud where he walked, here, in the post office, where Jurie Steyn's wife would complain about it."

Oupa Bekker shook his head.

"We know that Johnny Coen hasn't been around to the post office here since he heard that Pauline Gerber was coming back from finishing school," Oupa Bekker said. "And I think we can understand why. We know the kind of talk that there was about Johnny Coen and Pauline Gerber before Pauline suddenly decided to go to that ladies' school in the Cape, after all. If you remember, we said that Johnny Coen couldn't have been much of a young man if Pauline Gerber thought that going to a ladies' academy would be more exciting. Of course, we never said any of those things in Johnny Coen's presence –"

Thereupon Chris Welman remarked that since Pauline Gerber's return from the ladies' school in the Cape we hadn't seen much of Johnny Coen's presence.

It was almost as though Johnny Coen wasn't so much shy about seeing Pauline Gerber again, as that he was shy about seeing *us.* There was a thing now, Chris Welman remarked.

Oupa Bekker banged his tambotie walking stick on the floor, making small holes in the floor and sending up yellow dust. For the first time we realised that he was getting annoyed.

"You won't listen to me," Oupa Bekker said. "You'll never let me finish what I was going to say. Always, you just let me get so far. Then somebody says something foolish, and so I can't get to the important thing. Now, what I want to say is that At Naudé is quite right. And Johnny Coen is coming here. He's coming here this afternoon because he wants to know what *we* think. A young man in love is like that. He wants to know what we've got to say. And all the time he will be laughing to himself, secretly, about the things we're saying. A young man in love is like that, also. And his titivating himself, with the short blade of a pocket-knife and a handful of dry grass – well, you've got no idea how vain a young man in love is.

"And he's not making himself all stylish for the girl's sake but for his own sake. It's himself that he thinks is so wonderful. He knows less than anybody what she is like, the girl he is in love with. And it's only the best kind of pig's fat he'll mix with soot to shine his bought boots with. Because he's in love with the girl, he thinks he's something. Oh, yes, Johnny Coen will come around here this afternoon, all right. And what I want to say –"

At this point, Oupa Bekker was interrupted once more. But because it was Jurie Steyn who broke in upon his dissertation, Oupa Bekker yielded with good grace. The post office we were sitting in was, after all, Jurie Steyn's own voorkamer. There was something of the spirit of old-world courtesy in the manner of Oupa Bekker's surrender.

"— you, then, Jurie Steyn," Oupa Bekker said. "You talk."

Several of us looked in the direction of the kitchen. We

were relieved to see that the door was closed. That meant that Jurie Steyn's wife did not hear the low expression Oupa Bekker had used.

"What I would like to say," Jurie Steyn said, "is that I had the honour to drive Juffrou Pauline Gerber to her home in my mule cart, the day she arrived here at my post office, getting off from the government lorry and all –"

"What do you mean by 'and all'?" Gysbert van Tonder demanded.

Jurie Steyn looked around him with an air of surprise.

"But you were all here," Jurie Steyn declared. "*All* of you were here. Maybe that's what I mean by *and all*. I am sure I don't know. But you did see Pauline Gerber. You each one of you saw her. When she alighted here that day from the Zeerust lorry, on her return from the Cape finishing school. You saw the way she walked around here in my voorkamer, picking her heels up high – and I don't blame her. And her chin up in the air. And as pretty as you like. You all saw how pretty she was, now, didn't you? And the way she smelt. Did you smell her? You must have. It was too lovely. It just shows you the kind of perfume you can get in the Cape.

"And I am sure that if a church elder smelt her – even if he was an Enkel Gereformeerde Church elder from the furthest part of the Waterberge, I am sure that that Waterberg elder would have known that Pauline Gerber had class – just from smelling her, I mean. I am sure that that scent that Pauline bought at the Cape must have cost at least seven shillings and sixpence a bottle. Look at my wife, now, for instance. Well, I once bought my wife a bottle of perfume at the Indian store at Ramoutsa. And what I say is, you can *smell* the difference between my wife and – and Pauline Gerber."

Chris Welman, who had not spoken much so far, hastened to remark that there were other ways, too, in which you could tell the difference.

It was an innuendo that, fortunately enough, escaped general attention.

For it was Johnny Coen himself that came in at the front door of the post office at that moment. In one way, it was the

Johnny Coen that we had always known. And yet, also, it wasn't him. In some subtle fashion Johnny Coen had changed. After greeting us, he went and found a place for himself on a riempies-chair, sitting very upright.

He seemed from his manner to be almost unaware of our presence as he whittled a matchstick to a fine point and commenced scraping out the grime from under one of his fingernails.

Gysbert van Tonder, who always liked getting straight down to things, was the first to talk.

"Nice bit of rain you've been having out your way, Johnny," Gysbert van Tonder remarked. "Dams should be pretty full, I'd imagine."

"Oh, yes, indeed," Johnny Coen answered.

"Plenty of water in the spruit, too, I should think," Gysbert continued.

"Yes, that is very true," Johnny Coen replied.

"New grass must be coming along all right in the vlakte where you burnt," Gysbert van Tonder went on.

"Yes, very nicely," Johnny agreed.

Gysbert van Tonder grew impatient.

"What's the matter with you, man – can't you talk?" Gysbert demanded. "You know all right what I am trying to say. Have you seen her at all since she's been back?"

"I saw her yesterday," Johnny Coen said, "on the road near their house. I had to go quite a long distance out of my way to be *passing* there, at the time."

Gysbert van Tonder made a swift calculation.

"Matter of just under eleven miles out of your way, counting in the short cut through the withaaks," he announced. "Did she have much to say?"

Johnny Coen shook his head.

"Please don't ask me," he almost implored of Gysbert, "because I really can't remember. We did speak, I know. But after she had gone there was nothing we said that I could recall. It was all so different, after we had met, and we had spoken there by the road, and she had gone on back home again. It was all so different after she had gone. I wish I *could* remember what we said. What I said must have all sounded very foolish to her, I am sure."

Gysbert van Tonder was not going to allow Johnny Coen to get by so easily.

"Well, how did she look?" Gysbert asked.

"That was what I also tried to remember, afterwards," Johnny Coen declared. "How she looked. What she did. All that. But I just couldn't remember. After she had gone it was all just like it had been a dream, and there was nothing that I could remember for sure. She was picking yellow flowers there by the side of the road, she was, to stick in her hair. Or she was carrying a sack of firewood over her back for the kitchen fire, she was. And it would have been just the same *thing*, the way I felt. But I don't know. All I was able afterwards –"

"That was what I was trying to explain to them, Johnny," Oupa Bekker interjected, "but they never let me finish anything I start so say. They always –"

"Afterwards," Johnny Coen repeated, "after she had gone, that is, there was a kind of sweetness in the air. It was almost hanging in the air, sort of. Once I even thought that it might be a kind of scent, like what some women put on their clothes when they go to Nagmaal. But, of course, I knew that it couldn't be that. I mean, I knew Pauline wouldn't wear scent, I mean. She's not that kind."

"What I wanted to say earlier on, when you all interrupted me," Oupa Bekker declared, then, with an air of triumph, "is that a young man in love is like that."

New-year Glad Rags

"Uren, dagen, maanden, jaren
Vliegen als een schaduw heen."

The partition had been removed between the two classrooms. Ink stains and the marks left behind by water that had leaked through the thatched roof in the last rains were now covered up with a coating of whitewash. All the blemishes on the schoolroom walls of that year and of former years were hidden away.

For the more unhappy evidences of a year of educational activity within those walls the virginal film of unslaked lime served as both a mask and an immaculate cerement.

Dominee Welthagen had come over specially from Bekkersdal to hold an end-of-the-year service in that little bushveld schoolhouse that had for a night been changed into a place of worship.

Many of the desks were of the old-fashioned kind, seating a good number of pupils in a row, with the front parts detachable, so that their temporary conversion into pews had not presented much difficulty. There was that other, more modern kind of desk, however, with an iron framework, that obstinately continued to look like nothing else but standard Transvaal Education Department equipment, no matter what you did to it.

Nor did the blackboard standing on its easel in the corner take kindly to ecclesiastical disguise. Since this was a Calvinist service – and that sixteenth-century reformer's views on idolatry were well known – you couldn't go and hang an ikon, say, in front of the blackboard.

Maybe, if it had been a church service that Dominee Welthagen had come to conduct at some other time, the elders and deacons would not have been so energetic in altering the appearance of the schoolroom. But there seemed to be something about devotions arranged for the end of the year that called for a certain measure of stage setting.

After all, during the last few days of December one does, at times, become a prey to inner questionings. And it is only someone who is without human weaknesses of his own who will view with a cynical eye the earnest efforts of a deacon engaged in making a school cupboard look like an altar from the front. What is that thing inside the deacon – the cynic would ask – that the said deacon is trying to cloak? The answer, alas, is "many things". For there never has been a church deacon that did not have his share of frailties.

The young schoolmaster was, strangely enough, very helpful.

It wasn't often that the schoolroom was used for a church service. And, generally speaking, a schoolmaster was not too keen on that sort of thing. In the first place, the church authorities would obtain permission direct from the Education Department's head office in Pretoria to hold their service in the schoolroom, the schoolmaster's share in the formalities being limited to handing over the key of the building when an elder presented himself at the front door with a letter and a couple of Mtosa women carrying buckets of whitewash.

For the schoolmaster there was a certain amount of indignity in this situation.

All he would be able to say, reaching for his hat, was, "Well, I hope you won't slop all that stuff over my register again. Last year the inspector asked if there had been pigs at it."

Or the schoolmaster would say, unsmilingly locking some small change away in his desk, "Very well, you can take over. I've counted all the rulers and exercise books in the cupboard, there."

It wasn't that the schoolmaster was indifferent to the blessings that got conferred on the Groot Marico north of the Dwarsberge through these religious exercises. Indeed, when he thought of some of the church ouderlings he knew, he could only wonder where they would be, were it not for the benefits derived from divine intercession. Every schoolmaster who had ever taught in the Marico knew that church services held in the schoolroom did a lot of *good*.

But the trouble is that we all have our little human vanities. And the schoolmaster likes to think that in his schoolhouse he's a king. And so when a deacon, who is just an ordinary farmer, and with some of his children at that school, perhaps, turns up with a letter signed by somebody that's higher than a school inspector, even, why it stands to reason that that schoolmaster won't feel too bucked about it. Especially if the deacon has got a kind of a sneer on his face in the act of taking over.

But with the schoolmaster, young Vermaak, it was quite different, this year. Jurie Steyn's brother-in-law said so himself. And Jurie Steyn's brother-in-law was the deacon (an ouderling not being available at the moment, because of the ploughing) who had gone to young Vermaak with a letter signed by a high authority, requesting the use of the schoolhouse for the Almighty. We knew from that that the letter must have had a pretty high-up signature.

And Jurie Steyn's brother-in-law, the deacon, said that young Vermaak was ever so polite and friendly about it. It took away a good deal of his pleasure, at first, the deacon said. He had hoped to come into the classroom and to find the schoolmaster correcting a lot of examination papers, or filling in reports, and that the schoolmaster would have been very sarcastic about having to leave, the deacon said. He was looking forward to the schoolmaster walking out of the schoolroom in a nasty temper and asking when he was expected to do his work. And so, when the schoolmaster was, instead, helpful, he almost wished that he hadn't come along with that letter, the deacon said.

The deacon went on to explain that he made the Mtosas that he had brought with him lift the schoolmaster's table off the platform that it stood on, in front of the class. And young Vermaak didn't say a word. He even went to the assistance of one of the Mtosas who, forgetting for a moment that he was on a platform, stepped backwards off the edge of it, landing with his back part in a bucket of whitewash. The schoolmaster assisted the Mtosa with his boot, the deacon said, adding that he could not have done it more neatly himself, seeing that the Mtosa was sitting *in* the bucket of whitewash, and therefore not leaving much space, really, for getting properly assisted.

The schoolmaster went up a lot in his estimation, the deacon said, when he saw the quick way in which the schoolmaster helped that Mtosa to rise.

"And then I made the Mtosas stand the platform on its edge against the wall," the deacon added. "And they did that, one of them still limping a bit from the way the schoolmaster had helped him. And then I said I would cover the platform with those sheets of black drawing-paper that had pictures of mealies and maps of rivers on them. I said I would turn those drawings round and pin them onto the platform stood on its edge, and so it would look more like a *preekstoel,* the place where Dominee Welthagen was to stand.

"Those drawings had been made by young Vermaak himself, and they were stuck all round the walls. And I said it just for a joke, of course, in order to make him wild. And do you know what he did? He went and fetched a little packet of drawing-pins, so as to help us with that, also."

We were most surprised to hear that from the deacon. We were, after all, religious people ourselves. But we knew that there were limits. And we feared that if the schoolmaster got *so* religious, then it must be that there was something on his mind.

Then we remembered that we hadn't seen young Vermaak at Jurie Steyn's post office for quite a few months. Maybe that was worrying him, we thought – the fact that during all that time he hadn't come to visit us. But we also realised that, seeing it was drawing towards the end of the year, he would be too busy, setting examination papers and correcting them, and fixing things so that his favourite pupil would come first again.

Not that we bore him any ill will, on that account, of course. It was many years since any one of us had last been at school. And we were glad to think that we had been mellowed by the years, so that we no longer retained our childhood prejudices. We thought of a teacher's pet as a snivelling rat that wipes his nose on his sleeve, but we had no *evil* feelings about him.

"Snelt dan, jaren, snelt vrij henen
Met uw blijdschap en verdriet . . ."

It was beautiful the way we sang the words of the next verse of Hymn 160 in the schoolroom that had been converted into a house of worship, we all of us singing together.

This was a Reformed Church service. But that did not prevent quite a number of us who were Doppers from attending, also. Moreover, we who were Doppers were not allowed by our Enkel Gereformeerde Kerk to sing hymns; we were only permitted to sing psalms. And yet there was something about Dominee Welthagen's Reformed Church service that night that we couldn't resist.

And so in the end it was actually us Doppers who, strictly speaking, were not *allowed* to sing a hymn, even, that showed those Reformers how a hymn should be *sung*. But if only Dominee Welthagen had announced a psalm instead. If only Dominee Welthagen had said "The congregation will now sing 'Kom laat ons zamen Israel's Heer' – why, you would have heard us as far as Vleesfontein, and it would have been only Dopper voices that you would have heard, and Dominee Welthagen's own Reformed congregation would have been nowhere.

There was Jurie Steyn, there, wearing his new suit that he had bought by mail order, just sending his measurements. There was Oupa Bekker, with a collar that, if it was perhaps not quite so white, any more, as the predikant's, was certainly a good deal taller and stiffer. There was Gysbert van Tonder in a suit of formal cut, with a slit up the back of the jacket that was fashionable when Gysbert van Tonder first trekked into the Marico as a comparatively young man.

At Naudé was wearing his Sunday best, also a three-piece that, whatever its original colour, was now, except for a few undecided areas, an almost uniform green. Young Vermaak, the schoolmaster, looked dignified in navy serge. In that light you could hardly see the places where his landlady's daughter had cleaned the jacket with paraffin.

So much for the men in their New-Year apparel.

The women's dresses were, mostly, new. There was consequently little that, to the male gaze, would enable one frock to be distinguished from the next. With the women themselves, of course, it was different. They had a lot to whisper, behind hymn books, about skirt lengths and waistlines and hats – that was, if you could call a thing a hat that seemed to be a piece of cardboard with a blue handkerchief stuck on it with a brass safety pin.

But there were other words and other images, also, that some of the women whispering behind hymn books used in describing Pauline Gerber's hat. But afterwards they didn't talk about her hat so much . . .

"Welzaligh hij, die op U bouwt,
Geheel zijn lot aan U vertrouwt . . ."

We sang that at the end of the service, all of us standing up.

And it was only after the church was out that we started talking about Pauline Gerber, whom we hadn't seen much of since the time she had come back so smart and all, from finishing school. We said that she was looking smart as ever, now, no matter what you thought of her hat. We also started saying things about young Vermaak, the schoolmaster, then. We spoke of his singular behaviour in going away straight after the service, instead of staying to talk, first to one little group and then to another, in the way that we all did.

But mostly we spoke of Pauline Gerber. For by that time even the men, who were naturally not so observant in such matters as were the women, had noticed that, while Pauline Gerber's striped frock was no doubt styled to accord with the latest fashion, there was something in the actual fit of her dress that was obedient to a much older decree. It was well that her dress hung down wide like that, we said. It also struck us that, like young Vermaak, Pauline Gerber, too, had not stayed around outside the schoolhouse, to talk.

Black Magic

Naturally, we in the Marico are not superstitious. We do not believe in absurdities like sorcery and witchcraft, and all that. We accept a thing as a truth only after we have had proper evidence in support of it.

That is where we white people are different from the Mtosas, who will listen to anything that a witchdoctor tells them, no matter if it is a witchdoctor who is out of training, even, and has got to think first before he talks. Whereas a white Marico farmer would naturally laugh at information supplied to him by a witchdoctor, unless the witchdoctor could bring actual *proof* of what he was saying.

That was why Gysbert van Tonder was highly amused when a witchdoctor came round to his back door at the New Year and said that he had thrown the bones and had read in the bones something that was of great importance for Gysbert van Tonder.

The witchdoctor wore a flannel nightshirt with the skins of polecats sewn on it that seemed to need proper curing as much as the flannel nightshirt did. He carried his little bag of dolosse in one hand, and in his other hand he held a tattered umbrella.

And he wore spectacles. Taken all round, he was as proper-looking a witchdoctor as you see anywhere between the Dwarsberge and the Limpopo. What was more, he *smelt* like a good witchdoctor. Gysbert van Tonder noticed that part about the witchdoctor the moment he opened his back door to that knock that came at the New Year.

Well, Gysbert van Tonder is, of course, as far from superstitious as any man you can think of. But, as he admitted afterwards – talking about it in Jurie Steyn's voorkamer – when he smelt that witchdoctor at fairly close quarters, Gysbert van Tonder was to a quite considerable degree overawed. It was only when the witchdoctor started talking, however, that a broad smile came over Gysbert van Tonder's face.

For the witchdoctor said that he had thrown the bones in his hut on the previous night, and there had been a message about Gysbert van Tonder in the bones. Thereupon (having first requested the witchdoctor to stand a little to leeward of him) Gysbert van Tonder assured the witchdoctor in as affable a way as you liked that he now realised that what the witchdoctor had come round for was a New-Year present. There was consequently no need for the witchdoctor to have introduced make-believe – talking about having thrown the bones, and all that.

Gysbert van Tonder explained that to the witchdoctor in Sechuana, concluding his remarks with a quick downward movement of his left eyelid, a form of communication which, while it embraced, was not exclusively confined to, the language of the Bechuanas.

And because he was in a generous mood, this being the New Year and all, Gysbert van Tonder said to the witchdoctor that he could help himself to as much as he liked of the insides of a goat that Gysbert had but recently slaughtered, the said insides lying out there on a heap next to the stables.

Of course, Gysbert van Tonder would have been kind like that to a witchdoctor in any case, the New Year or not. Even though you may not be superstitious, it is always as well to keep on the right side of a witchdoctor. You never know.

So you can imagine how surprised Gysbert van Tonder was when the witchdoctor did not appear at all grateful. With a wave of the umbrella he had in one hand, the witchdoctor explained that he hadn't called round just for a dinner. He didn't wish to take up much of Baas van Tonder's time, the witchdoctor said, because he knew what a busy man Baas Gysbert was.

And what disconcerted Gysbert van Tonder somewhat was that, when the witchdoctor made that remark, he saw fit to imitate Gysbert van Tonder's bit of pantomime of earlier on. The witchdoctor's left eyelid fluttered swiftly down onto the top part of his wrinkled cheek.

Gysbert would – as he said to us afterwards – in the ordinary course of things have kicked the witchdoctor for that. Or for less than that, even. What restrained him, Gysbert van Tonder said, was that it was still the season of goodwill – even though it was a few days late, perhaps – and the fact that he didn't like getting too near the witchdoctor, in spite of the wind blowing in the other direction.

It was then that the witchdoctor informed Gysbert van Tonder about what he had seen on the previous night, when he had thrown the dolosse in his hut, the moon being at the half.

"The way the bones fell, Baas Gysbert," the witchdoctor said, "I could see a ghost talking to Baas Gysbert. I think the ghost was Baas Gysbert's grandfather or Baas Gysbert's great-grandfather, even. He was very old. And I knew by the ghost's feet that he was of Baas Gysbert's family. The ghost had the same kind of feet as what Baas Gysbert has got – big and with the same kind of flatness. Has Baas Gysbert got a grandfather or a great-grandfather, perhaps, that is today a ghost?"

Gysbert van Tonder started getting annoyed. His eyes travelled to his veldskoens, which he contemplated thoughtfully for a few moments.

"You got pretty big feet yourself," Gysbert remarked to the witchdoctor, then. "Flat, too. About as flat as any feet I've ever seen. Anyway, how can you tell all that rubbish from just throwing a sackful of bones? If it wasn't that it's New Year, and it's therefore a sin to do it, I'd set my dogs onto you. I've got an old Boer bulldog that's chased just about everything in his time. He'd be glad of the chance of chasing a witchdoctor, also, while he's still got proper teeth. Even if my feet are maybe a little what you call flat, you've got no right to come and talk to me like that at the back door of my own farm."

The witchdoctor said then that he was sorry, and that he didn't mean it that way at all. It was only that the elderly ghost with . . . with that kind of feet was explaining where the money was hidden. And so he thought it was his duty to come and tell Gysbert van Tonder about it. The witchdoctor was still going on, apologising some more, when it suddenly dawned on Gysbert what he had been saying.

"Money?" Gysbert van Tonder ejaculated. "What's that you've been saying about money? Look, never mind about the insides of that goat. I'll give you a piece of the goat itself. It's more than I and my family can eat, and goat doesn't keep too well in this weather. But what's that you've been saying about money?"

"It's about where the money is hidden –" the witchdoctor repeated. Then he suddenly stopped and took a step backwards. The Boer bulldog that Gysbert van Tonder had been talking about had come sidling up from behind the water tank and was sniffing at the witchdoctor's pole-cat skins.

It was evident, from the way he was growling, that the Boer bulldog was displeased about something. Gysbert van Tonder acted quickly. The Boer bulldog streaked off in the direction of a clump of camel-thorns, yelping. The witchdoctor wiped some stray beads of sweat from his forehead.

"Au," the witchdoctor said, glad that he was not being chased. There was something about the easy loping gait of the Boer bulldog that you could not but admire.

"You dirty, lazy brute!" Gysbert van Tonder shouted out after the retreating bulldog. Then, turning to the witchdoctor, he said: "I got him a good one, didn't I? I'm glad I stopped him before he could bite a piece out of you. He frightened you a bit, though, I'm sure."

Suddenly an idea occurred to Gysbert van Tonder.

"I'll tell you what, seeing it's the New Year, and all," Gysbert said – and before he realised what he was doing, his left eyelid again came down in a swift wink – "what would put you right would be a little . . . you know, just a little . . ."

"Yes, thank you very much, my baas," the witchdoctor said. "Yes, please, just a little."

And this time, when the witchdoctor winked, Gysbert van Tonder was not so very annoyed, somehow.

After the witchdoctor had downed at a single gulp what was in the pannikin that Gysbert van Tonder had fetched for him out of the black jar in the kitchen, the two men stood looking at each other for some moments in silence. Gysbert van Tonder didn't quite know how to reopen the subject.

"What . . . what the ghost was saying, now . . ." Gysbert began, and coughed.

He found himself restrained by an unwonted sense of the fastidious. It was strange how squeamish they had become in their conversational intercourse, the white man and the Bechuana witchdoctor. It was as though the unseen powers that institute African taboos had already got to work, prohibiting the free use of certain consecrated words.

First, the witchdoctor couldn't talk about feet without Gysbert van Tonder getting hot under the collar. Then, as though by common accord, both Gysbert van Tonder and the witchdoctor refrained from mentioning that what the witchdoctor had drunk out of the pannikin was apricot brandy – and, what was more, was good apricot brandy.

And now, finally, Gysbert van Tonder couldn't bring himself to talk about money, just straight out. It is well to keep away from the black arts. They get you enthralled before you know where you are.

Gysbert van Tonder coughed again. "The ghost with the big . . . I mean, that rather old sort of ghost," Gysbert van Tonder started again. "That ghost, you know, that you were talking about. He mentioned something that was hidden, somewhere, I think you said . . ."

"Oh, yes, the money, Baas Gysbert," the witchdoctor said, his face lighting up with intelligence and apricot brandy. "Oh, yes, the money that is buried here on Baas Gysbert's farm."

So much Gysbert van Tonder enlarged onto us about his first meeting with the witchdoctor at the New Year. There were certain things, too, that he left out, but that we, sitting in Jurie Steyn's voorkamer, could guess.

Gysbert told us that he had already dug in several places, and pretty deep, too, sometimes.

Mostly, it was at the foot of trees. But there were other places, too, where he had dug. Like right under the bakoond at the side of his house. That was a pretty deep hole, Gysbert van Tonder commented, and because of the crack that came into the bakoond through that, the bakoond wasn't so good for baking bread in, any more, although it might perhaps still do for the more ordinary sort of cooking.

"But surely you didn't go just by what the witchdoctor *said*," At Naudé enquired. "I mean, you must have asked him for *proof*. How do you know that he wasn't just telling a lot of lies?"

But Gysbert van Tonder had a proper answer to that. He said that At Naudé must not think that he was just an ignorant Mtosa. He interrogated the witchdoctor all right, Gysbert said, but the witchdoctor was able to *prove* that the bones he had in his sack were the very same bones that he had thrown in his hut the night he threw the bones. What was more, the witch-doctor said he could still go and point out in his hut to Gysbert van Tonder the exact place where he was *sitting* on the floor of his hut, at that time.

We agreed that that was convincing enough.

"I've given the witchdoctor a few goats, since then," Gysbert van Tonder said, after a pause. "Live ones, I mean, that he can take back home with him, when he leaves. And you know, I sometimes almost wish that he *would* go. I have dug so many holes, already . . . I don't know. It sometimes looks like just a waste of time to me."

Thereupon Chris Welman asked what the trouble was. Why couldn't the witchdoctor just take Gysbert to the right place – that was, if there *was* a right place – Chris Welman wanted to know.

"That's it," Gysbert van Tonder said, "that's the whole difficulty. The witchdoctor says that the ghost didn't talk very distinctly. And that was another thing that made me believe that the witchdoctor was telling the truth. After all, a ghost *wouldn't* talk too distinctly. But there was another reason also, why I believed the witchdoctor."

And we knew what that reason was, of course. And we knew that Gysbert van Tonder would never mention it. Because that would inevitably call to mind the unhappy *nom de guerre* of Doors Kalkoenvoet that, because of his slab-like pedal extremities, Gysbert van Tonder's grandfather had borne with him to the grave.

"I know the witchdoctor is doing his best, of course," Gysbert van Tonder resumed. "But I'll tell you how I felt the other night. It was the night when I got out of bed to fetch an eiderdown out of the loft for him, because he was complaining of the cold. I felt that I should rather have kicked the witchdoctor, that day, than my Boer bull."

After Gysbert van Tonder had left we said, discussing the matter among ourselves, that black magic, as practised by Bechuana witchdoctors, was indeed an awful thing.

"As far as I can see," Jurie Steyn observed, "Gysbert van Tonder guessed right the first time. All the witchdoctor came round for was a New-Year present. And it seems he got it, all right."

Oupa Bekker sniffed.

"Giving him a goat, too," Oupa Bekker said. "Well, it looks to me that, whoever the goat is, in all this, it's not the witchdoctor."

Laugh, Clown, Laugh

"It's the clown," Johnny Coen said, starting to laugh all over again. "The tall clown in the fancy dress – yellow and blue and the smart way of walking. I could go to the circus and see it all through again, just to laugh at that clown. He kept a straight face even when they chucked the bucket of water over him. It was a real scream to see his new clothes getting all soaked . . . oh, *soaked*. And he went on standing there in the middle of the ring as solemn as you like, not being able to make out where the water came from, even."

Johnny Coen laughed as though he were seeing all that happening again, right in front of his eyes, and for the first time.

But Oupa Bekker said that what he liked best at the circus were the elephants. The way they stood on their hind legs and the way they walked on bottles, Oupa Bekker said, balancing themselves to music.

"It's years ago since I was last able to balance *myself* to music," Oupa Bekker continued, "leave alone walk on bottles."

"Or stand on your hind legs," Jurie Steyn commented – not loud enough for Oupa Bekker to hear, though.

In the old days there wasn't any such thing in the Transvaal, Oupa Bekker went on, as walking on bottles. Even though the whole of the Marico up to the Limpopo was elephant country in those days, Oupa Bekker said – and, in consequence, he prided himself on knowing something of the habits of elephants – he would never have imagined their walking on bottles.

If an elephant had seen a bottle in his path he would simply have walked over it. To him an elephant in those days was just an elephant, Oupa Bekker said.

And the same thing applied to lions, when the Groot Marico was lion country, Oupa Bekker added. To him a lion was just a *lion*, and not a bookish person that . . . that, well, we all saw what those lions *did* at the circus, didn't we, now? There was more than one white man in this part of the Marico that wasn't nearly as well-educated as some of those circus lions, Oupa Bekker said.

Of course, he acknowledged that not every white person in this part of the Marico had had the same opportunities of schooling as the lions had had.

Then At Naudé said that what he just couldn't get over, at the circus at Bekkersdàl, were the trained zebras.

"And to think that this was also zebra country," At Naudé remarked. "But I would never have imagined a zebra wearing a red ostrich feather on his head, just like he's a Korana Hottentot. Or a zebra, while galloping down to the water-hole, first stopping to write something on a blackboard with chalk."

We spoke also about other animals that we had seen at the circus, and we said that the Groot Marico had at one time been that kind of animal's country, too. And all the time we had never known what those animals were really like. That sort of thing made you think, we said.

When Jurie Steyn was talking about the mule we had seen at the circus, that could jump six feet, and Jurie was saying that the Groot Marico was also mule country, Gysbert van Tonder suddenly gave a short laugh.

"And the clowns, that Johnny Coen was mentioning," Gysbert van Tonder said. "Well, it seems to me that for a pretty long while the Marico has been good clown country. And still is."

We were more than a little surprised, at a remark like that coming from Gysbert van Tonder. And several of us told him that we thought he should be the last person to talk. We proceeded to give Gysbert van Tonder some sound reasons, too, as to why we believed he should be the last person to talk. And some of the reasons we gave him had to do with things that hadn't happened so long ago, either.

This discussion would probably have gone on for quite a while, with each of us being able to think up a fresh reason every few minutes, when Chris Welman started talking about the fine insouciance with which the red-coated ringmaster had cracked his whip.

The ringmaster hadn't looked very particular as to whether it was the gaily caparisoned horse he hit, or the blonde equestrienne hanging head downwards from the saddle, her golden locks trailing in the sawdust – so it had seemed to Chris Welman, anyway.

"She didn't once stop smiling, either," Chris Welman said, "all the time the music played."

From the way Chris Welman spoke, it was apparent that, in the sounds given forth by the circus band, his ear had detected no harsh dissonances. Nor to his eye had the set smile of the equestrienne conveyed any suggestion of artifice. It was, however, significant, that in his unconscious mind he had, indeed, established a link between those two circus reciprocals – the music's blare and the set smile.

"After the circus was over and I had got back home, I was still thinking of her a long time," Chris Welman said. "I thought of her a good way into the night. I thought of her with the electric light on her hair, hanging down on the ground, and her spitting out the sawdust every time that it came into her mouth from the way she was riding, hanging down."

It was obvious that Chris Welman had occupied a ringside seat.

"But mostly I thought of her, about what she was doing after the show was over," Chris Welman said. "I pictured her there under that tent, locked up alone in her cage. It must be an unnatural sort of life, I thought, for a girl." And he winked.

We were able to put Chris Welman right on that point, however.

It wasn't that we had any sort of inside knowledge of circus life, of course, but we just went by common sense. It was only the more wild kind of performers in a circus that got locked in cages, we said. The tamer ones just got knee-haltered, we said, or tied to stakes with riems. So he was quite wrong in thinking of the blonde equestrienne as having to be locked in a cage after the show was over, we told Chris Welman. Likely as not they even let her go loose, we said. And we also winked.

Thereupon At Naudé said that that was the trouble.

And after we had pondered At Naudé's remark carefully, we realised that there was much truth in it.

A pretty girl, we said, if she was wild enough, was a lot more dangerous than any kind of lion. Because all a pretty girl needed to do was to lower her eyelashes in a particular way, we said. And for that she did not have to be an equestrienne or an equilibriste or anything else, we added.

It was only natural, after that, that the talk should turn to the subject of pretty girls in general. And it was still more natural that, before we knew where we were, we should be discussing Pauline Gerber.

What made it somewhat difficult for us to talk as freely as we would have liked, about what we had been hearing of Pauline Gerber lately, was the fact that Johnny Coen was there, sitting in Jurie Steyn's voorkamer.

And we knew full well how Johnny Coen had felt about Pauline Gerber, both before she went to the finishing school in the Cape, and after she came back from the finishing school.

As it happened, however, Johnny Coen helped us out, to some extent, and perhaps without knowing it, even.

Gysbert van Tonder had just made the admission that, in so far as he was able to judge, Pauline Gerber was not only the prettiest girl in this part of the Marico bushveld, but also the most attractive. "If you know what I mean by *attractive*," Gysbert van Tonder had added. "Otherwise I could tell you –"

That was when Johnny Coen had interrupted Gysbert van Tonder.

"No, no, you don't need to tell us," Johnny Coen said, hastily, "not in words, and all that. And not when it's – when it's Pauline Gerber, I should say. You've told us things like that before today. About what you find attractive in girls, that is. And so if you perhaps don't say it all over again, we won't feel that we have missed anything. Because you've said it all *before*, that is."

After a few moments' reflection, Gysbert van Tonder conceded Johnny Coen's point. He had spoken on that subject quite a good bit, he acknowledged, but there was still just this one thing he wanted to say.

"Not now, please," Johnny Coen interjected. And he spoke so sharply, and with such unwonted heat, that Gysbert van Tonder shut up, looking slightly puzzled, all the same.

"I was only going to *say* . . ." Gysbert van Tonder concluded in an aggrieved tone, and left it at that. For if Johnny Coen was going to act funny, and so on, well, it was not a matter for him, Gysbert van Tonder, to have to go out of his way to help Johnny right.

"Well, I've only seen Pauline Gerber a few times, since she's been back from finishing school," Johnny Coen said. And from the way he said "few" we knew that he wanted us to think that it meant more than, say, exactly twice.

But, of course, we weren't really interested in the number of times that Johnny Coen had seen Pauline Gerber of late. What we were anxious to learn was how often the young schoolmaster, Vermaak, had been seeing her. For it was in relation to young Vermaak, and not to Johnny Coen, that a certain amount of talk was going on about Pauline Gerber.

"Well, the few times that I have seen her," Johnny Coen went on, "it was a bit difficult for me to know what to think, exactly. The first time I saw her the schoolmaster had just left. And the second time – I mean, on *another occasion* when I saw her at her house, she was sort of expecting Meneer Vermaak to come round. But what I want to say is that what Chris Welman said about the circus girl – why, that is exactly what I *feel* about Pauline Gerber. About how pretty she is, and all that. And what makes it still more queer is that she talks about herself like Chris Welman talks about the girl that rides in the circus.

"She feels she's shut up in a *cage*, Pauline Gerber says. To have to live here in the bushveld, with everybody so narrow-minded, Pauline Gerber says, is like being shut up in a cage."

Johnny Coen went on at considerable length, after that, acquainting us with the true nature of the sentiments he entertained for Pauline Gerber. But we were not interested. We did not in any way doubt the purity or sincerity of his feelings. Only, we were not concerned with all that. What we really wanted to know was what was going on between Pauline Gerber and the young schoolmaster. And it was apparent that

Johnny Coen couldn't tell us more than what we already knew. It was a pity that Johnny Coen should be struck with such blindness, though, we thought. It would be better if the scales were to drop from Johnny Coen's eyes, we felt.

It was Oupa Bekker who brought the talk back to a discussion of the circus – which was, after all, where we had started from.

"Walking *on* bottles," Oupa Bekker was saying. "Well, that's a new one on me. And I knew the Marico when it was elephant country. Unless, maybe, it was giraffe country. And what a giraffe would look like, standing on his hind legs, I just can't think of, right away."

That was what gave Johnny Coen his chance to get back to the clowns, once more.

"The one clown poured water from a stepladder out of a bucket onto that other clown that I was telling you about," Johnny Coen said. "And I just about laughed my head off, each time, to see how that other clown got soaked. And they had Natives to come running in from the back entrance with more buckets of water. And it all went over that clown. I enjoyed it more than I enjoyed the Chinese acrobat, even, who jumped through two wheels with knives in them. And all the time that clown didn't know what was happening. Every time I saw a Native come running in with another bucket of water, why I just about *died*, laughing."

We gazed at Johnny Coen pretty steadily, as he spoke. And we thought of what was going on between Pauline Gerber and young Vermaak, the schoolmaster. And all the time Johnny Coen went on feeling the way he did about Pauline. And we wondered if Gysbert van Tonder had been so far wrong, when he said that this was clown country.

The tears started coming into Johnny Coen's eyes, eventually, the way he was laughing about that clown.

Anxious to Hear

It was not that young Vermaak, the schoolmaster, was not talking with his usual confidence, and all that, sitting in Jurie Steyn's voorkamer. And as always, he was pretty sure of his facts. Moreover, the subject we were discussing – namely, the visit to the Marico of Dr Lesnitzky, the archaeologist – was just in the young schoolmaster's line.

And yet, if you knew him at all well, through having met him at intervals over a considerable period, you could not but detect that young Vermaak was not entirely at his ease, even when he spoke most learnedly.

And we noticed that when Oupa Bekker asked him a question about Pauline Gerber – Oupa Bekker making the enquiry in what you might call a quite pointed way – the constraint in the schoolmaster's manner showed no visible diminution. It got worse, if anything.

So much so, indeed, that Gysbert van Tonder, speaking in a chummy, man-to-man fashion, advised him to cheer up. The schoolmaster bridled. And not unnaturally. You couldn't help it, but there always would be something brutal, sort of, in the sound of Gysbert van Tonder instructing anybody to cheer up.

"I don't know what you're getting at," young Vermaak informed Gysbert, speaking to him coldly, as though he were a standard three pupil that had got a simple fraction sum wrong. "I'm only discussing the fossilised footprints of the Jurassic period that Dr Lesnitzky has discovered in the bed of the Malopo. What you mean by saying that I should cheer up about it, I just don't understand. They aren't my footprints –"

The schoolmaster glanced around the voorkamer, as though expecting us to laugh. It was evident that he had made what he thought was a clever remark, and that he expected us all to laugh, whereby Gysbert van Tonder would be shown up as somebody very ignorant. As it happened, however, we didn't laugh. There had been quite a lot of talk about Pauline

Gerber and the schoolmaster, here in the Groot Marico. And it wasn't the kind of talk that you could just dismiss with a laugh. Especially if there was any truth in what the women thought they had observed about Pauline Gerber, the time they saw her at the church service held in the schoolhouse at the end of the year.

For that reason, we were prepared to believe quite a few things about the schoolmaster. If there was one thing that we had reason to suspect him of – why, there could just as well be another thing. It was not unlikely that Dr Lesnitzky had found out something else about young Vermaak.

"In the Jurassic *slime* . . ." the teacher continued, trying to make it sound still funnier.

Yes, that was about right, we thought. If Jurassic was like *that*, well, we were less provoked to laughter than ever. Maybe Dr Lesnitzky had got hold of something, we thought, if he was making remarks like that about the schoolmaster.

"Mind you, it's not that I *blame* you for anything," Gysbert van Tonder declared, sententiously. "You'll find that nobody here *will* blame you for anything. Not as long as you do the right thing, that is. I mean, we are all men. We all know how a young fellow can get – can get tempted and all that. But we expect you to act square. As for what that Professor Lesnitzky says about you and the Jurassic slime – well, *that* you can forget about. You can take it from me that nobody in the Groot Marico will ever hold that against you. It's the sort of thing that could happen to anybody, I should imagine. That part of it you can just forget about."

The past was nothing, Gysbert van Tonder said, it was *now* that mattered.

This time it was Gysbert van Tonder's turn to look around him, his eyes travelling from face to face. And each one that Gysbert van Tonder looked at nodded his head in agreement, each of us sitting there in Jurie Steyn's post office.

"Yes, old chap," At Naudé said to young Vermaak, talking to him comfortingly, "don't you take any notice of that Dr Lesnitzky. He's a foreigner, in any case. I mean, what does he really know, what's going on in the Groot Marico? Let him say anything he likes about you and the Jurassic slime you've been talking about. That's something he'll have to prove in court. And you can take my word for it that we're with you. We'll stand by you, and we'll make that Dr Lesnitzky look silly. It's only that other thing, you know –"

The schoolmaster brushed aside At Naudé's remarks with a gesture. And he spoke to At Naudé in a much haughtier way than he had done to Gysbert van Tonder. Never mind standard three, he addressed At Naudé as though At Naudé had just that morning come to school for the first time, and At Naudé didn't know a thing, and he was snivelling there, thinking of the place at the spruit where he made clay oxen with the Mtosa piccanins. The schoolmaster spoke to At Naudé as though At Naudé had all the feelings that a bushveld youngster has when he comes to school that first day.

"Do you know what the Jurassic slime is?" the schoolmaster demanded of At Naudé.

"No," At Naudé replied, "but I've a pretty good idea. And all I can say is that that Dr Lesnitzky needn't talk. He's got a good bit of it on himself, too, if you ask me. I wouldn't be surprised if some of his own footprints are there, also, and not just yours. He looks that sort –"

Well, that was when the schoolmaster was able to give a short laugh, in which there was no mirth – and in which there was no implied invitation for anybody else to join in, either. It was the kind of laugh that a person has on his own, and is glad to have that way.

And when he started talking, the schoolmaster was really able to spread himself. Several of us felt that it was a mistake to have given him that opening. For there was no doubt that this was exactly up young Vermaak's street, and so he just let himself go.

He told us things about geology, that we had never known existed, until then. And he said that the footprints Dr Lesnitzky had discovered in the bed of the Malopo River were so ancient that it was quite ridiculous even to try and work out *how* old. Hundreds of thousands of years, the schoolmaster said. Millions of years, even.

And while they did not look unlike human footprints, except that they were maybe on the small side, no human being could have made them, since they were stretched too far apart for any human to have walked or even run like that.

"The Jurassic is only a geological formation," young Vermaak went on. "It is quite ridiculous to suggest the idea that there is anything *unpleasant* about it. It comes in between the Cretaceous and Triassic groups and includes the Oolite and the Lias. It is a formation rich in fauna."

Young Vermaak went on at great length. And he spoke almost with his old self-assurance. It was as though he felt that, on the dry bed of the old Malopo, he was on safe ground.

There were no quicksands, there, that he could get trapped in. While he stayed on the Jurassic side of the Malopo's dried-up bed he was beyond the reach of any present-day criticism that we could level at him, sitting there in Jurie Steyn's voorkamer. Even the Cretaceous was millions of years before Jurie Steyn's voorkamer, the schoolmaster explained.

"Abounding in echnidons," young Vermaak was saying.

Well, when it was that sort of talk, the ordinary bushveld farmer was just nowhere. And we realised that. We had no hold on him. The schoolmaster could go on talking until the lorry from Bekkersdal came, and after that, as long as his information on the Triassic lasted out. And from the Triassic he would be able to switch to something else, no doubt.

We had no means of making contact with a man sitting on a riempies-stoel millions of years away, and taking it easy. If it came to the worst, the schoolmaster would also be able to recite those mineralogy tables that he knew by heart.

And we were satisfied that it made him happy to do that, too, seeing how seldom we gave him the opportunity for it.

But it was when Oupa Bekker cleared his throat, and a far-off light came into his eye, that we knew that young Vermaak would not have it all his own way, any more, for much longer. That light in Oupa Bekker's eye spoke, somehow, of battle – a battle in some forgotten war, long past, that Oupa Bekker had taken part in when he was still young.

"Those footprints in the Malopo," Oupa Bekker said, "well,

I've seen them. Only, that isn't the Malopo, of course. It's only an arm of the Malopo. If your Dr Lesnitzky doesn't know that, you can tell it to him from me. The Malopo itself flows on past Tweedepoort. And I've never known a time when there wasn't water in that part of the Malopo, that you're talking about – in the arm there hasn't been water in living memory."

When Oupa Bekker said "living memory" it seemed to be something that went back so far – further than the Jurassic, even, somehow – that more than one of us felt a little uncomfortable. Chris Welman coughed too, then.

"Now, this Jurassic, that you're talking about," Oupa Bekker asked the schoolmaster, "has it got anything to do with Jurie Steyn? I'm only asking, of course. You see, I don't know much about what has been happening in these parts, lately. Things up to war with Sekukuni I can remember very well.

"It's only things that happened later, like Jameson's Raid, for instance, that I don't remember so clearly. Today I can't remember any more the name of the Mshangaan woman that Jameson borrowed the white apron from that he held up, at Doornkop. But is this Jurassic that you're talking about called after Jurie Steyn?"

Jurie Steyn leant forward over his post-office counter, for a moment, looking hopeful. You could sense what Jurie Steyn was feeling, too. It was as though, for a brief spell, Jurie Steyn was wondering whether, after all, he had perhaps not lived in vain. With the schoolmaster's next words, however, Jurie Steyn resigned himself to an acceptance of the common fate of all of us mere mortals.

"What do they want to call *anything* after Jurie Steyn for?" young Vermaak asked. For the schoolmaster had just been talking geology. Consequently, his concern for the factual overrode those human considerations that find their expressions in diplomatic utterance.

"I mean, it would be silly, wouldn't it," young Vermaak went on, "to go and give Jurie Steyn's name to some part of the science that deals with the condition and structure of the earth. Think of how absurd it would be to call one of the geological strata –"

Since he had no pretensions to being anything more than human, Jurie Steyn could stand only so much. All right, the Jurassic system wasn't called after him. Good, he accepted that. For that matter, he had never really expected anything else. He knew only too well – and from his own experience, what was more – how blind the world could be when it came to according a person the just due for his merits.

It was like the time the Government auditor came from Pretoria and said that Jurie Steyn's post-office accounts were all mucked up, and the Government auditor just wouldn't listen to all that Jurie Steyn had to tell him about the Mtosas dressed in old blankets that came to buy stamps and about the trouble he was having in the milking shed with his new separator. Jurie Steyn *knew* that the world was like that.

But for that young schoolmaster to come and sneer at him now, Jurie Steyn thought, and all for nothing. Well, the cheek of it. In any case, he wouldn't be in the schoolmaster's boots for anything. Surely, the schoolmaster must know that Pauline Gerber had a father who in single combat with a bergluiperd (and with only two dogs to help him) twisted that bergluiperd's left foot off. And Pauline Gerber also had an elder brother who had once bitten . . . But no, Jurie Steyn would rather not think of that. All he felt was that he wouldn't for anything be in young Vermaak's shoes. Not with the relatives Pauline Gerber had, that was.

And there was the schoolmaster talking in a sneering way about the impossibility of geological science having named something or other after him, Jurie Steyn. Maybe geological science *had* named that thing after him, Jurie Steyn thought, and he hadn't come to hear of it, yet, seeing how slow news from the outside world was in reaching the Marico bushveld.

Jurie Steyn leaned further than ever over his post-office counter, then.

"Whatever Oupa Bekker is going to say," Jurie Steyn announced, "I'm certain he's *right*."

"Of course, I'm right," Oupa Bekker declared, sure of himself but at the same time trying not to look self-satisfied. "I tell you, I've seen those footprints. And Jurassic my foot . . . I was almost going to say my footprints. But how old did you say they were, Meneer Vermaak?"

The schoolmaster told him. Jurassic, the schoolmaster said. Hundreds of thousands and millions of years. What you could practically call Mesozoic, the schoolmaster said, rolling the word appreciatively over his tongue. And the distance that those footprints were apart. It was obviously before man. Some being akin to man, maybe. They had a lot in common with a human being's footprints, all right. And the Jurassic was also rich in ammonites and cycads.

Oupa Bekker gave a short laugh, this time, that no one joined in.

"I never saw who made those footprints," Oupa Bekker said. "But I saw them. And I recognised them right away as Bushman footprints. And if you want to call a Bushman a human being, well, that's up to you, of course. I'm not saying anything. And why they are still there, in the arm of the Malopo, those footprints, is because there hasn't been any rain, there, for over a hundred years. No real rain, that is.

"And why those footprints are so far apart is because that was just the time when the percussion cap came in, to take the place of the flintlock that the old Boers used in their voorlaaiers. And with the percussion cap in, and all, it was only natural that the Bushmen would *have* to take longer strides. I mean, much longer strides than when it was just an old flintlock that he was trying to get away from. Has your Dr Lesnitzky ever thought of that one?"

And so Oupa Bekker put young Vermaak in his place, all right, Jurassic or no Jurassic. As we knew that Oupa Bekker would, of course, the moment we saw how his eye glittered. We were all very pleased to see the schoolmaster brought back to earth – and back to the present – out of his millions of years ago. *Now* let young Vermaak try and explain away a few immediate things, we said to ourselves. Let him try and explain about Pauline Gerber, for one thing. We were willing – and even anxious – to hear.

That was when Jurie Steyn's wife came in from the kitchen with our coffee. And to our surprise she was most kind to young Vermaak. It was something we couldn't understand, somehow. The way she told him not to worry, when she handed him his coffee. It was as though she knew all about Pauline Gerber, and forgave him for it. It was as though she forgave him much . . .

The way Jurie Steyn's wife spoke to young Vermaak, you would almost think that it was *he* that was in trouble.

"For the way you're feeling now," Jurie Steyn said to At Naudé, "if you want my advice, I'd say you should go somewhere where you can get away from civilisation, for a bit. Nerves, that's what you've got. Why don't you go on a fishing trip to the Malopo for a week? You know – get right away from things."

Chris Welman had another suggestion to make.

"If you want my advice," Chris Welman said to At Naudé, "you'd go and camp for a while at the Bechuanaland end of the Dwarsberge. That's almost on the edge of the Kalahari. You've got no idea how desolate that part is. It's a howling wilderness, all right.

"You've got to be there only a day or two, and you'll forget that there ever was such a thing as civilisation. You could even take Gysbert van Tonder along with you. That should help your state of mind a lot. With Gysbert around, the lower end of the Dwarsberge would look absolutely barbaric. Gysbert has got that effect even on a city, I mean."

Somehow, Gysbert van Tonder did not seem quite as pleased as he might have been at the subtle flattery conveyed in Chris Welman's speech.

"You go and –" Gysbert van Tonder started ungraciously. Then he bethought himself.

"Ah, well," he ended up. "I suppose one can have too much of civilisation. And I am quite willing to believe that that is At Naudé's trouble – his listening in to the wireless and reading the newspapers every day. His brain has got too active. But you can be glad that that is a kind of sickness that you will never suffer from, Chris Welman."

Gysbert van Tonder seemed very pleased with himself, the way he made that remark.

Strangely enough, the friendly controversy in which Gysbert van Tonder and Chris Welman saw fit to indulge did not tend to allay any of the restlessness with which At Naudé's spirit was charged.

For At Naudé acted in what we could not help feeling was a quite singular fashion. First he half rose to his feet, emitting a long moan. Then he suddenly slumped back again into his riempies-chair, at the same time smacking the open palm of his right hand in a despairing manner against his forehead. His visage was noticeably contorted.

"All the same old childishness," At Naudé exclaimed, "that's supposed to be clever or that's supposed to be funny. I can't stand it any more, this heavy what's assumed to be Marico *fun*. If it's not Jurie Steyn doing it, it's Chris Welman. Or it's Gysbert van Tonder. And if it's not Jurie Steyn's wife, it's Oupa Bekker or it's *me*. And if it's not me, it's – oh, I tell you it's driving me mad. And when I switch on the wireless it's the same thing. It's either the Free State Monday Jokers or it's the Tuesday Choir of Comical Ouderlings or it's the Wednesday Half Laughs with the Upington District and Schweizer-Reneke/Kaokoveld Trek-Boers.

"And then, when I try to escape from all that, and I come here to Jurie Steyn's post office to fetch my letters, what do I hear but somebody saying, 'That's a good one, ha, ha, ha!'"

It was clear to us that At Naudé was in a bad way. Gysbert van Tonder opened his mouth to say something, but Oupa Bekker nudged him to silence. We all felt that an unreasoned remark, at that moment, could have a very adverse effect on At Naudé. And we also knew that it would be no unique thing for Gysbert van Tonder to *make* an unreasoned remark. It was best that At Naudé should be allowed to talk himself out, we felt.

Some time in the future, making use of diplomatic skill, we would be able to point out to him, talking as man to man, the dangers to which he exposed himself, sitting day after day in his voorhuis alone, reading the newspapers and listening in to wireless programmes. If At Naudé went on like that much longer, he would become somebody learned before he knew where he was.

And where would At Naudé be then, in this part of the Groot Marico, if he had learning? Just nowhere, we felt.

"Another idea," Gysbert van Tonder suggested, "would be for you to go and pitch a tent alongside the Crocodile River. It's quiet enough there. At least one of the banks is quiet, the one where there isn't much grass on. No, on second thoughts, I don't think you should go there. Because you might just by mistake pick the wrong bank – the one that the Crocodile River gets it's name from. You'd be surprised how busy things can be on that side, in the season."

So Oupa Bekker said that if it was civilisation that At Naudé wanted to get away from, well, there was Durban. He had been to Durban only once, Oupa Bekker said, but it was enough. It was quite a story, too, how he got to Durban, in the first place, Oupa Bekker added. But Durban was quite a good place to go to, if you were sick of civilisation.

"The same old thing," At Naudé remarked to Oupa Bekker. "And I know exactly what you're going to say, too. It was the old days. And you went there by mule cart. Or you were a transport driver, and you went there by ox-wagon. And on the way back you gave a young student of divinity a lift as far as Kimberley.

"And years later you saw the young student of divinity's photograph in a newspaper. And he was a bit older then, but not much, for the years had treated him kindly. And then you realised, for the first time, that the young divinity student with the handsome side whiskers that you had given a lift to from Durban was Solly Joel. I don't know how often I haven't heard that kind of story."

When we spoke about it afterwards, we said among ourselves that the expression on At Naudé's face was quite fiendish.

"And if it wasn't Solly Joel," At Naudé continued, "it was some other Rand millionaire. And if it wasn't a student of theology or a Sunday-school superintendent – but no, it *had* to be. It couldn't be anything else. Without that, you old-timers wouldn't think there was any point to your stories.

"I mean, I've never heard of any of you transport drivers giving a lift as far as Johannesburg to an Australian doing the three-card trick. But you must have, otherwise, how could they have got there? No, it's either Solly Joel, or Wolff Joel or Lionel Philips or Sammy Marks – and they were doing nothing all the time but thumbing lifts on ox-wagons between Durban and the Rand.

"When did the Rand mining magnates find time to float their companies, then? Or time to have a bath in champagne – like we know they did? I tell you, it's more than a year, now, that I've been listening in to every wireless programme that's got somebody talking about life in South Africa in the old days. And you'd be surprised how many of them are transport drivers.

"It must have been a very healthy life, I should think, driving a heavily loaded ox-wagon from the coast to the Transvaal, before there was a railway. And sometimes, when one of these old transport drivers says that what he was bringing up from Durban was a big consignment of dynamite – and the announcer starts asking him questions over the wireless – I begin to hope.

"But it turns out, in the end, that it really was a healthy life. They had no trouble with the heavy load of dynamite to speak of.

"But there was a religious-looking young man with handsome side whiskers that the transport driver had given a lift to. And that young man became the chairman of a mine that ends with the word *Deep*. And a Johannesburg suburb is today called after him. And that whole load of dynamite, from the coast to the Rand, didn't as much as singe the young theologian's side whiskers. You see, it's not that I don't like Oupa Bekker. My trouble is just that I've heard him before, and so often.

"There isn't a day passes but I hear something like 'Uit die Ou Dae' over the wireless. Or 'Toeka se Tyd', or 'So Het die Ou Mense Gelewe', or 'Ja-nee'.

"And I get sick of it. I just can't help it, but I do. And when . . . when I come here and sit down in Jurie Steyn's post office, and I hear Oupa Bekker talk of the old days, and I realise that he didn't have any trouble with cases and *cases* of dynamite, either (I mean, otherwise he wouldn't be here), well, it isn't that I wish Oupa Bekker any harm, you understand.

"But I've heard everything he's got to say. Every time Oupa Bekker speaks it sounds to me as though he is being introduced by a wireless announcer, and as though there is somebody playing the piano for background effects. I mean, Oupa Bekker isn't real to me, any more.

"Even the way he spits behind his chair – well, it looks to me like a *put on* sort of spit, if you know what I mean. I don't feel that Oupa Bekker is spitting just because he's got to."

We looked at At Naudé in amazement. It was clear that he was in a pretty bad way. There was no telling how far this sort of thing could go. We felt that we wanted to help him, if we could. The next thing he would do, he would start crying, and right here in front of us. And all because of his nerves. We had seen just that same thing happen before, to a stranger from the city.

The stranger had been with us for quite a while, and was really trying to understand us, and the things going on in our minds. And he was taking notes, even. And then one day – just like that – he started crying. We felt that At Naudé was going the same way, through too much civilisation that he was getting over the wireless and from reading newspapers.

It came as a relief to us – for At Naudé's sake – to hear Oupa Bekker's voice once more.

"The last time I went to Durban wasn't in the old days, but two years ago," Oupa Bekker said. "And why I said that it was like a story was because I went there by train. I had never before in my life travelled so far by train. And that was a wonderful thing for me. Because I would never have believed, otherwise, that you could journey so far by train. We didn't once have to get out and walk. Or change to a postcart. Or mount a horse ready saddled that would take us along a bridle path over the worst part of the *rante* –"

"Then it couldn't have been in the Union," Chris Welman shouted out, trying to be *really* funny. "You couldn't have been travelling on the S.A.R."

We were pleased that Oupa Bekker ignored Chris Welman.

"No trouble over the whole journey," Oupa Bekker continued. "It was only when I got off at the station and a Zulu came and pulled my suitcase out of my hands. But I had never in my life seen a Zulu like that. He had bull's horns on his head and seashells on his feet. That was just how my grandfather had told me that the Zulus were dressed at Vechtkop."

We laughed at that, of course. After all, those of us who had been to Durban knew that about the Durban ricksha pullers – the way they dressed up to look ferocious. But all they did was to transport you and your luggage to an hotel.

"That sort of talk," At Naudé began, his lip curling, "and I suppose when you got to the hotel –"

"That's why I say that Durban is so uncivilised," Oupa Bekker explained. "Because it was only when we got to the hotel that the ricksha puller started apologising for all the boot-polish brown that was coming off his chin. He was working his way through college, he told me. He said it was steadier work than looking after babies or mowing lawns, the sea-shells on him rattling as he spoke. He was a divinity student, the ricksha puller said."

Go-Slow Strike

When At Naudé, who reads the newspapers, came into the post office he was wearing a wide grin.

"Ha, ha," he said to Jurie Steyn, who was leaning forward with his elbows on the counter. "Don't tell me, Jurie. I know why you're standing like that. You're on a go-slow strike. Ha, ha."

Jurie Steyn gazed at At Naudé uncomprehendingly.

"The newspapers say that it's not an official go-slow strike," At Naudé went on, laughing some more, "but of course, you've joined it, haven't you, Jurie? We all know you started before the others. Years before, I should say. I mean, ever since this post office was opened here . . ."

"Go-slow strike?" Jurie Steyn enquired blankly. "First I've heard of it. What do they want a thing like that in the post office for? Especially when I'm having all this trouble already with the new mealie-planter."

In a few words At Naudé acquainted Jurie Steyn with the latest news, which had to do with the go-slow strike that the post office employees were staging.

Jurie Steyn was indignant. "Well, if that's what the Postmaster General wants me to start doing now, on top of everything else," Jurie Steyn said, "then I say he can keep his job. Let the Postmaster General come over here and look at my new mealie-planter with the green paint on it. If he still wants a go-slow strike after that I'll tell him he can go and sit down outside and have it on his own. My wife can take him out coffee."

Thereupon At Naudé explained to Jurie Steyn that a go-slow strike was not an additional duty imposed on a bushveld postmaster by the Postmaster General. Indeed, as far as he knew, the Postmaster General was not even in favour of the go-slow strike that the post-office employees were taking part in. For that matter, he doubted if the Minister of Posts and Telegraphs himself was terrifically keen on it, At Naudé said.

Before Jurie Steyn could take it all in, however, Gysbert van Tonder was saying that he had also bought one of those new mealie-planters. In consequence, we all started talking animatedly, several of us at the same time.

More than one farmer from the far side of the Dwarsberge had purchased one of those new mealie-planters after having had it demonstrated in front of the hardware store; the demonstration consisting of the shop assistant filling the seed hopper with mealies and the farmer pulling the mealie-planter up and down on the stoep so that he could see how it worked, the mealies falling out just the right distance from each other with the way the wheels turned; and the farmer enjoying himself.

"Up and down, up and down I went on Policansky's stoep," Gysbert van Tonder said. "I promised David Policansky that I would be careful and not knock any of the new green paint off his mealie-planter. But he said just go ahead. Just make myself at home, he said. He would send somebody along later on to sweep up the mealies I had sown on his stoep, he said. I was not to worry at all.

"Well, I went on until about midday, and by that time I was perspiring quite a lot, because that mealie-planter gets quite heavy to pull, after a while, and the stoep of the hardware store was inches deep in mealies, the way I had been sowing them.

"And then, when it was about midday, to judge by the sun, a whistle blew somewhere – at the sawmill, I think – and Policansky came out of his store and said he thought I could knock off now for lunch. Everybody was knocking off for lunch now, Policansky said."

Chris Welman was able to confirm Gysbert van Tonder's remarks in a considerable measure.

"I just about laughed my head off, too," Chris Welman said, "on Policansky's stoep. How that mealie-planter could drop seeds at any distance you wanted – because you can adjust it, too, you know."

So we all said, yes, we knew you could adjust a mealie-planter. That was when the trouble started. If it didn't start even before then, At Naudé commented, sombrely.

"That's just the point," Chris Welman continued. "The mealie-planter doesn't seem to work so well on the lands, behind a plough, going over kweekgras sods and pieces of turned-up ant hill, as it does on the smooth stoep of Policansky's hardware store. It doesn't work nearly so well, I mean. With its new green paint and all, what does a mealie-planter do, as likely as not?"

Meanwhile, Jurie Steyn had put a further question to At Naudé.

"Are you sure you read it right, At?" Jurie asked. "What it said in the newspapers, that is? Did it say all that about the go-slow strike? You know, you have been wrong once or twice . . ."

"Once," At Naudé admitted. "I know you're thinking of the time when I came and told you about the money for the Kunswedstryd that got stolen, that I had read about in the Bekkersdal newspaper. But then it came out afterwards that it was a mistake the printer had made in the newspaper."

Several of us spoke up for At Naudé, then. Because we remembered the circumstances. And so it wasn't At Naudé's fault at all for having given us incorrect information. It was just what he had read, about the Kunswedstryd funds getting embezzled. But Dominee Welthagen wrote to the newspaper about it, and what Dominee Welthagen wrote was so strong, we said that even a lawyer couldn't have done it better. And he got an answer right away from the editor. And the editor was very nice about it, the way he explained that it was all a mistake made by the printer. We all said afterwards that the editor of the newspaper couldn't have acted any more handsomely than he did, how he put all the blame on the printer.

And we said that it would be a good idea if, before he just wrote a thing, a printer went and made sure of his facts first.

And what made the whole thing still more peculiar was that there actually *wasn't* any money for the Kunswedstryd, that year.

"Yes, that mealie-planter, green paint and all, wasn't nearly as clever at the bottom end of my turflands," Gysbert van Tonder said. "I'll go so far as to say that for that kind of soil the old-fashioned way of getting a Mtosa to walk behind the plough and stick each seed mealie in with his finger is even better. Yes, I really think that when it comes to the stickier sort of black turf, then a mealie-planter is less educated than a Mtosa."

We felt that was a sweeping statement. Gysbert van Tonder sensed our thoughts.

"I know it doesn't *sound* right what I've just said," Gysbert continued, "but I'm only talking about turf soil, mind. I know that a mealie-planter with its shining wheels *looks* much more clever than a Mtosa just arrived for work in the morning from his hut. And I won't say that a mealie-planter hasn't perhaps got more human feelings, also, than a Mtosa. I'm not arguing about that, see?"

What Gysbert van Tonder insisted on, however, was that on turf soil you had to hand it to a Mtosa for education.

"What's more, a Mtosa doesn't need to paint himself all green," Gysbert van Tonder added, as though that clinched the case. "All a Mtosa puts on himself, at a Ndlolo dance, say, is perhaps a little white and blue."

"But does it mean I've got to work slower, right here in my voorkamer?" Jurie Steyn asked of At Naudé while the rest of the conversation was going on.

"Yes, that's the idea," At Naudé replied. "You've got to work only half as fast. It's for more pay."

Jurie Steyn's eye gleamed.

"More pay, hey?" he repeated. "Well, there's a thing for you, now. You'd imagine you'd get less pay for working only half as fast, wouldn't you? But I suppose it all goes to show. You've got to know these things."

At Naudé nodded.

"Yes, it's no good being ignorant, like what Gysbert van Tonder says that mealie-planter is – more ignorant than a Mtosa even, Jurie," At Naudé acknowledged. "You've got to know what's going on. The newspaper I got this morning says just why those unofficial leaders of the post-office workers decided to take this kind of action."

Jurie Steyn said that was a good one, too, if you liked.

"Calling it *action*," Jurie Steyn said. "When what they mean is *less* action. When they mean that I've got to do just half as much action, here in my voorkamer, that is. They should call it *un*-action, rather, I'm thinking."

Gysbert van Tonder's voice sounded very loud, all of a sudden.

"– a whole piece with no mealies at all," Gysbert van Tonder was saying. "And then a short stretch with every single seed in the hopper planted into it. And planted in such a way that you can't get the mealies out again, unless you go down on your hands and knees and scrape."

Thereupon Chris Welman said that they should have a machine for doing that, also.

"A machine for scraping out the seeds that have been sown in the wrong place," Chris Welman said. "The mealie-unplanter you could call it, I suppose. That would be a funny thing, now, wouldn't it? Useful, though."

But Jurie Steyn said that it was no more funny than what At Naudé had just told him. It was, indeed, similar.

Then, when the lorry driver's assistant came in with the mailbags, Jurie Steyn attended to him with an air of studied leisureliness. And Jurie Steyn opened only one mailbag.

"The rest of your letters, kêrels," he said, indicating the second mailbag, which he had placed under the counter, "I'll let you have tomorrow. I get more pay if I do it like that."

Nor did the latest intelligence, as supplied by the lorry driver's assistant – to the effect that the go-slow strike had been called off – make any impression on Jurie Steyn. Half-speed and more pay was quite good enough for him, he said. He asked for nothing better. He could keep it up longer even than the Minister of Posts and Telegraphs could, Jurie Steyn reckoned.

Circumstantial Evidence

One story we heard was that Pauline Gerber's eldest brother, Dons, spoke to young Vermaak, the schoolmaster, on the platform at Zeerust station. According to this story, the schoolmaster was just getting ready to board the train, and Dons Gerber had a single-barrelled shotgun in the bend of his arm when he spoke to the schoolmaster.

According to the second story we heard, young Vermaak was sitting in the classroom, after school, correcting exercise books, and it was Pauline Gerber's youngest brother, Floris, who addressed him, Floris oiling the mechanism of a Mott-Mauser at the time.

It was difficult to know what to believe, exactly. Each story was so well authenticated. The circumstances relating to Dons and the railway platform embraced the language that the train guard used when he had to stop the train, after having blown the whistle, so that the schoolmaster could get his suitcases out of the compartment again.

"It's how a ticket examiner spoke to me, once," Gysbert van Tonder observed, "when I was travelling on a mail train to De Aar. I may say that I didn't have a ticket at the time that the ticket examiner addressed me."

If they weren't exactly *alike*, Gysbert van Tonder added, the ticket examiner's words still bore a family resemblance to the expressions employed by the Zeerust train guard in advising the schoolmaster to make up his mind.

Thereupon At Naudé was also able to recall a less happy travel experience of his own, that had to do with his ejecting an empty half-jack of brandy from a train window at Rysmierbult. He never knew where that empty half-jack *got* the ganger, exactly, At Naudé said, but he could still remember how the ganger who happened to be on the line at the time complained about it for the full twenty minutes that the train halted at Rysmierbult.

"By the timetable, the train should have stopped there only ten minutes," At Naudé proceeded, "but I think that why there was that long wait that day was because the engine driver got a respect for the ganger's language, after listening to it for a bit, and so he felt he wanted to give him a bit of a show. I won't say that the ganger didn't take full advantage of the extra ten minutes that the engine driver allowed him, either. All the same, I still wonder, today, where that bottle did hit the ganger."

On the other hand, the other story, which had to do with Pauline Gerber's youngest brother, Floris, seemed to be quite as well-appointed in respect of circumstantial detail.

For the railway platform's strident bustle you had only to substitute the scholarly calm of the Drogedal schoolroom with its thatched roof and whitewashed walls, the pupils, their text-books cast aside, having long since departed, on foot or by school donkey cart.

The only sounds in that peaceful classroom, with the day drawing to its close, would be the even scratchings of the schoolmaster's red-ink pen in double-ruled exercise books supplied by the Transvaal Education Department.

At intervals, the schoolmaster's pen would *slash*, somewhat, and there would be a measure of unsteadiness about the schoolmaster's breathing. But those were matters readily to be understood. Mistakes in composition and sums. But, I mean, infamous mistakes.

And then, very suddenly, there would obtrude the click-click sound of the bolt mechanism of a Mauser being operated. It was a situation not wanting in drama. After all, we all know why a Mauser has got to be oiled so often. Its magazine system lacks the smoothness of the Lee Enfield.

You can't fire an old Mott-Mauser as fast as a Lee Enfield, maybe. But over 800 yards aimed at a person running, it's more accurate.

Nevertheless, Jurie Steyn said that it seemed rather a silly thing for Pauline Gerber's youngest brother, Floris, to have done – going along oiling his gun there in the classroom.

"Why couldn't he have done all that at home?" Jurie Steyn

wanted to know. "He must have been a bit soft in the head, if you ask me. Perhaps he still is."

But Chris Welman said he did not think that Jurie Steyn was well-advised in making that particular kind of remark. Not where Pauline Gerber's youngest brother was concerned, Chris Welman said. Or her eldest brother, either. Or even any of her in-between brothers.

Perhaps it would have been best if Jurie Steyn had merely said that Pauline Gerber's youngest brother had been a bit playful, walking into the classroom with a gun *and* an oil-can, and if Jurie Steyn had then just left it at that. Perhaps that was all Jurie Steyn *wanted* to imply, Chris Welman suggested, his voice sounding very gentle, all at once.

Jurie Steyn bridled.

"If you think I'm scared of the Gerbers, old Koos Gerber or any one of his sons, or the whole lot of them together, even," Jurie Steyn announced, "then you don't know me, that's all. A lot of loud-mouthed braggarts, that's all they are. Bullies, too, if you ask me. Cowards, that's what."

But Gysbert van Tonder reminded Jurie Steyn that on the railway platform Pauline Gerber's eldest brother, Dons, had said hardly a word. It was the train guard that did all the talking. It was the train guard that you could say was perhaps loud-mouthed, Gysbert van Tonder said. Telling young Vermaak to hustle with his traps, and what to do with his umbrella.

Similarly, in the classroom of the Drogedal school, Chris Welman interjected, Pauline Gerber's youngest brother, Floris, had said nothing at all.

"As far as we *know*, Floris Gerber didn't talk," Chris Welman said. "Of course, I don't suppose he had any need to talk, exactly. Working on the bolt of the Mott-Mauser was taking up all his attention, I suppose, and if he spoke he might have spilt some of the oil over the school books."

It was clear, however, that Chris Welman had got Jurie Steyn going. Maybe even Chris Welman himself, when he had in a spirit of bushveld perversity hinted to Jurie Steyn not to speak out of his turn where the men of the Gerber family were involved – maybe even Chris Welman had not counted on so complete a success for his stratagem.

"The more I think of this whole business," Jurie Steyn declared, "the more my heart warms to young Vermaak. The way that young schoolteacher has been treated here, in the Groot Marico, just because he's a stranger. All I can say is that it's un-Christian."

There was something for you, now.

It took our breath away. We tried to remember over how long a while Jurie Steyn had regularly gone out of his way to make the schoolmaster feel small. And just because, as we all knew, Jurie Steyn's wife had a soft spot for the schoolmaster.

And yet a few simple words spoken by Chris Welman (Chris Welman having done nothing more than to impugn Jurie Steyn's physical fortitude when faced by the Gerber brothers) could have the effect of changing Jurie Steyn's outlook in a single moment.

Here was Jurie Steyn actually declaring, for all of us to hear, that he was siding with the schoolmaster. That gave you some idea as to how scared Jurie Steyn must be of the Gerber brothers, all right. His next remark bore it out even more clearly.

"I only wish I had Dons Gerber and Floris Gerber right here in front of me now," Jurie Steyn announced, sticking out his chest. "I'd let them know where they got off, all right. But, of course, they never come round here. They pretend it's because Post Office Welgevonden is nearer, for them. But I know that's not the only reason.

"I know it's because the postmaster at Welgevonden is too soft. He allows himself to be put upon, by bullies."

We felt that, after those remarks of Jurie Steyn's, there was very little that we ourselves could say. We had no more to say than what Dons Gerber had had to say on the Zeerust railway platform. We could express our thoughts in less words than what Floris Gerber had employed in the classroom at Drogedal.

That was when Johnny Coen started taking a hand in the conversation.

"Doesn't it strike you, at all," Johnny Coen asked, "that it can't both be true, these two different stories about how the schoolmaster came in the end to ask Pauline Gerber to marry him? Don't you think it's possible that perhaps *both* those stories are lies, I mean."

We were shocked to hear Johnny Coen using language like that.

Naturally enough, we were quite willing to make many sorts of allowances for Johnny Coen. For one thing, we knew perfectly well how Johnny Coen had been feeling about Pauline Gerber. We realised, also, that he had entertained those sentiments about Pauline Gerber long before she had ever set eyes on young Vermaak, the schoolmaster.

But we also knew that Pauline Gerber had been to finishing school, in the meanwhile, and so it was only reasonable that things should no longer have been the same between Pauline Gerber and Johnny Coen, after she came back to the Marico. For, if she did feel the same way about Johnny Coen, it would mean that all the money that her father had spent on her at the finishing school at the Cape had been wasted.

Johnny Coen appeared to sense the constraint in Jurie Steyn's voorkamer then, following on the statement he had just made.

"I don't mean to say that you're all of you just a lot of — liars," Johnny Coen said, giving utterance to a couple of words that the train guard had also found useful on Zeerust station. "I don't mean that at all."

So Gysbert van Tonder said to Johnny Coen that we were grateful to him for that, he was sure.

"It's not that," Johnny Coen persisted, half-ashamed of himself for having put it so impolitely. "But what I mean is, if young Vermaak was on the Zeerust railway station, with Dons Gerber with him, then who was sitting in the classroom marking copy-books in red ink, when Floris Gerber was there?"

"I mean, they couldn't both of those things be true, could they, now? The next thing you'd be saying is that it was Floris Gerber sitting at the table marking the standard five spelling mistakes in red ink. That would be a muck-up, *wouldn't* it?"

The thought of that provoked Johnny Coen to laughter. We smiled indulgently. Only Oupa Bekker seemed to think that Johnny Coen did have something there. He himself didn't believe either of these stories about how young Vermaak came to ask Pauline Gerber for her hand, Oupa Bekker said.

"Jolliest passengers we've had in a good while," the lorry driver's assistant remarked, walking into the voorkamer with the mailbags. "Laughing all the way up from Bekkersdal."

So Chris Welman said that he supposed it was more of those Native convicts that were coming to work at Derdepoort.

"But what they've got to laugh about I don't know," Chris Welman continued. "And yet that's what I always think, when I see those Native convicts sitting in the lorry in their striped jerseys – laughing their heads off about something. And the warder with them looking so miserable, you feel you want to go and ask can't you do something for him."

"No, not convicts, this time," the lorry driver's assistant said. "Only Pauline Gerber and her brothers, Dons and Floris and – I forget the names of the other two –"

"Out there in the lorry?" Jurie Steyn enquired, looking not too comfortable suddenly.

"No, they got off at Welgevonden," the lorry driver said. "And, of course, young Vermaak was with them, too. You know, he's engaged to Pauline. They went to Bekkersdal to celebrate."

The lorry driver looked surprised at the question Gysbert van Tonder put to him.

"How did the schoolmaster propose to Pauline Gerber?" the lorry driver repeated. "Well, what do we all do? He rode over to the farm, one afternoon, and asked her father, of course. And Oom Koos Gerber shook him by the hand and said he wanted a young man to help look after the farm – as though he didn't have enough already, with all those sons he's got. But why did you ask?"

Thereupon Gysbert van Tonder said, no, it was nothing. It was just something Jurie Steyn had been mentioning, Gysbert van Tonder said.

Border Badman

Gysbert van Tonder was talking about the new young mounted policeman who had gone galloping past while he and Frits Nienaber were outspanned alongside of the government road, a few days before. It was partly at the off mule's suggestion that they had outspanned at about that spot.

"The off mule stood right up on his hind legs," Gysbert van Tonder said, "to show us how tired he was. We knew that the next thing the off mule would do, would be to drag the mule cart off the road and right up the side of the koppie, and with nobody to help him, either. For the steeper a koppie is, the better that mule likes to drag a cart over it, when he's real tired.

"And that new policeman on border patrol didn't even notice us," Gysbert van Tonder said. "We could see that he was in a hurry to get somewhere. He didn't even see the mule, I don't think. Of course, he's new –"

Then Oupa Bekker mentioned another occasion on which a border patrolman came and assumed duty in the Marico for the first time.

"Of course, I am talking of very long ago, now," Oupa Bekker said, "and the patrolman's name was Duvenhage, and we could see that they had explained to him in Pretoria that his most important work would be to put down the awful cattle smuggling that was going on here, in those days."

"Oh, yes, in those days, of course," Gysbert van Tonder said, quickly.

Jurie Steyn took Gysbert van Tonder up at once.

"What do you mean by saying 'in those days', like that?" Jurie Steyn asked. "What about that bunch of cattle with wide horns and all colours that you've got in the camp by the kloof, there, right now? I suppose you'll tell us next that you bought them on the Johannesburg market. And how's it Frits Nienaber has about the same-looking collection of beasts on *his* side of the kloof? One thing I must say, is that the two of you seem to have divided up pretty equally. You seem to have been honest there, anyhow."

"And I expect that's why you keep that herd in the kloof," Chris Welman observed to Gysbert van Tonder sarcastically, "it's because they are a sort of cows and oxen that don't like to have people come prying into their affairs."

"Especially when they've still got Bechuanaland Protectorate clay between their hooves," Jurie Steyn remarked. "Turf clay."

So Gysbert van Tonder said that they would have to prove it. And so Jurie Steyn told us what he would have done if he had been a border patrol policeman instead of a postmaster. And then Gysbert said that if Jurie Steyn sorted out hoof prints in the dust like he sorted letters in his post office then you could bring Bechuanaland cattle across the Convention line in broad daylight.

Thereupon Oupa Bekker said what a queer thing it was that there should be so much jealousy among Marico farmers.

"I mean there isn't one of us wouldn't smuggle in a few head of cattle if he got a chance," Oupa Bekker said, "and yet when you hear of your neighbour doing it – and you yourself didn't do it, that time – and you picture to yourself a herd of all sorts of cattle crowded against the barbed-wire fence on one side of your neighbour's farm and sniffing the wind from the Protectorate, and lowing, why, you get pretty mad about it. It's almost like you're also pawing the *polgras* with your hooves, sniffing the wind that blows from Bechuanaland."

We could not but admit that there was much truth in Oupa Bekker's words. At the same time – as Chris Welman pointed out, then – there was such a thing as overdoing this cattle-smuggling business. And it was people that overdid it that gave all Marico farmers a bad name, he said.

Gysbert van Tonder sniffed. It was a different type of sniff from the kind Oupa Bekker had been talking about.

"A bad name," Gysbert van Tonder said, his lip curling, "well, there are some people sitting here in this voorkamer now that would give any district that they stayed in a bad name, just by living in it. If they lived in the Cape Peninsula, it would get a bad name. And you can't tell me there's any cattle smuggling going on in the Cape Peninsula. Unless you can smuggle in cattle off ships."

Gysbert van Tonder grew thoughtful after that last remark. It was as though he was considering the possibilities.

"But there was a thing, now," Oupa Bekker said, getting back to the subject of Patrolman Duvenhage, of the old days, "I mean, the Justice Department sending a man who had been on the Illicit Diamond staff at Kimberley to come and keep watch on the Transvaal border. I suppose the Transvaal Government thought that a man who had had a job like that in the Cape must know a thing or two. They didn't want somebody just raw, I suppose.

"Well, I'll say this much for Duvenhage. There wasn't much smuggling being carried on by Marico farmers during the time he was a patrolman. Only, he didn't stay here very long after there was that trouble about the railway consignment notes."

Chris Welman said that although he knew it had all happened very long ago, he did have some sort of recollection of it. It was like something he had been told in his childhood.

"Wasn't Duvenhage the patrolman that was caught smuggling quite a big herd of cattle across the border?" Chris Welman asked. "With his police boys helping him? I seem to remember something about it. The police boys were singing Bechuana cattle songs, the white policeman joining in."

"Yes, the same," Oupa Bekker replied. "And I still remember my first meeting with him. He asked me *where was their hang-out.* And when I said I didn't know what he meant, he said the cattle-smuggling kings. The heads in the game, he explained. He wanted to know where they sat talking and drinking."

Oupa Bekker said that he could see from that that Patrolman Duvenhage's training on the Illicit Diamond staff in Kimberley had been of such a nature as to leave him somewhat out of touch with conditions in the Groot Marico bushveld.

"I mean, I couldn't go and tell him that there wasn't such a thing as a gang of foreign cattle smugglers working in these parts," Oupa Bekker said. "After all, we all know that if there is such a thing as a few head of cattle being brought across the line on a night when there isn't much of a moon, well, then we know it can be almost any Marico farmer trying to do a bit of good for himself.

"And we know that there is no particular place where that Marico farmer will go and sit and drink and talk about it, afterwards.

"The only place where a Marico farmer might have a drink would be in the Zeerust bar at Nagmaal. And then he would only talk about the crops, or about the Dominee's sermon, or about how he's got the laziest bywoner on this side of the Dwarsberge, and that that bywoner has got the impudence to be making eyes at his daughter."

Oupa Bekker went on to explain the details of a piece of strategy that he and his partner, Japie Krige, had thought up to get Patrolman Duvenhage out of the way on a night when they were going to smuggle cattle into the Transvaal.

"I wrote a note to Japie Krige," Oupa Bekker said, "and in the note I told Japie Krige exactly where he had to be at Derdepoort, at midnight, with the wire-cutters.

"And Japie Krige helped me to write the letter. And we laughed quite a lot. We laughed especially at that bit in the letter where I said how careful Japie Krige had to be of that new patrolman, Duvenhage, because he was such a fine asset to the force and had eyes like a hawk.

"We were laughing to think of how proud Duvenhage would be of himself when he read that letter. Then we explained to a Mchopi messenger how he must walk past the police station in a suspicious way, so that Patrolman Duvenhage would be sure to arrest him, and find the letter on him."

In the meantime, Oupa Bekker said, he would be sitting quietly at home, and his partner, Japie Krige, would be driving cattle towards the boundary fence, and at the right moment a Bechuana would come and call him, and in the starlight they would cut the barbed wires of the fence and bring the cattle across.

And during all that while Patrolman Duvenhage would be lying in the veld, miles away, at Derdepoort, next to a swamp. And why Patrolman Duvenhage would be thinking all the time of his bed at the police station, while he was lying by the swamp, was not because of the pillow on the bed, but because the bed had a mosquito net round it.

"But that evening," Oupa Bekker said, "when it was not a Bechuana from Japie Krige that came to my door, but Patrolman Duvenhage, then I knew that there was something wrong."

All the same, Oupa Bekker said, he could tell by Patrolman Duvenhage's manner that he had not come to arrest him.

"Duvenhage walked straight into my voorkamer and didn't even take his helmet off," Oupa Bekker said. "And when my little yellow brak pup snapped at him, Patrolman Duvenhage landed out one with his boot that sent the yellow brak pup flying through the door and then it travelled about a hundred yards up the road before it turned around to let out a yelp. I could tell from those signs that Patrolman Duvenhage didn't have a case against me."

So Gysbert van Tonder said, yes, he knew. It was when a border patrolman came to your house and was polite, that you had to watch out. It was when a patrolman patted your youngest son on the head, and asked him what class he was in – professing surprise that he should be so far advanced with his education – that the next thing the patrolman would say to you was to get your jacket.

Oupa Bekker said that Patrolman Duvenhage had come pretty straight to the point.

"After that Mchopi messenger had crawled about four times through the same stretch of thorns behind the police station," Patrolman Duvenhage said to Oupa Bekker, "I decided to give him a break. So I went up to him and kicked him twice, and told him to hand over the letter. Because I knew that was what he wanted. I mean, it's an old stunt on the diamond fields."

Oupa Bekker said he could see, from that, that there was an unkind streak in Patrolman Duvenhage. Thinking it was funny to let that Mchopi go on crawling through the thorns all that time, when he could have gone and dealt with him right away.

But it was when Patrolman Duvenhage started talking about how much there would be in it for himself, that an unhappy note crept back into the conversation, Oupa Bekker said. For Patrolman Duvenhage spoke very emphatically about what he called a rake-off, a word Oupa Bekker had not heard of, until then.

"When Japie Krige arrived about midnight with the herd of smuggled cattle, the drovers singing the chorus of a Bechuana cattle song," Oupa Bekker went on, "Japie Krige came into my voorkamer prepared to be very indignant because I had not assisted him at the fence.

"But when he saw who it was, sitting opposite me at the table, Japie Krige turned very white. And I have never seen a man hide a pair of wire-cutters behind his back quicker than what Japie Krige did then. But Patrolman Duvenhage did not even bother to look up from the figures that he was working out on a piece of paper.

"But one thing I will say is that Japie Krige and I never brought any more cattle over the line while Duvenhage was the patrolman. We just couldn't I mean. Patrolman Duvenhage's percentage of rake-off, that he worked out for us on paper, was too high. In the end, the only man left in the business *was* Patrolman Duvenhage. I often wondered how it was that he came to lose his job in Kimberley, though."

In the silence that followed, Jurie Steyn seemed to be doing a bit of quick thinking.

"What you said at the start," Jurie Steyn said to Gysbert van Tonder, "about you and Frits Nienaber there by the roadside, last week, and this new policeman riding past, and him not seeing you. Maybe it was that you didn't want him to see you, I'm thinking. I suppose you were hiding in the bush, you and Frits Nienaber."

Gysbert van Tonder asked Jurie Steyn what gave him that idea.

"The Bechuana cattle in your camp by the kloof," Jurie replied. "And this new policeman riding so fast. And I can guess where he was going to, as well – yes, to Derdepoort. All the same, I'd like to know what you said about him in the letter to Frits Nienaber that the policeman took off your messenger."

"I wrote in the letter," Gysbert van Tonder declared solemnly, "that Frits Nienaber must be on his guard, because the new policeman was a fine asset to the force and had eyes like a hawk. And to think that he rode right past us, on his way to Derdepoort, and didn't even see the off mule."

Monument to a Hero

We all said afterwards, talking about it in Jurie Steyn's voorkamer, that the unveiling of the monument erected to the memory of Hartman van Beek had been a most impressive ceremony. We felt privileged to have been present at a great and unforgettable occasion, we said, talking like some of the speakers at the unveiling.

"What I think was the best was Dominee Welthagen's address," Chris Welman started to say, when Jurie Steyn interrupted him.

"What about the Volksraad member's words?" Jurie asked. "There was something for you, now. How the Volksraad member said that at last and after many years we were honouring the debt we owed the memory of Hartman van Beek, rearing a pillar of plain granite –"

"That was like Hartman van Beek's own life had been, strong and plain," Chris Welman interjected. "But Dominee Welthagen said that also."

So Jurie Steyn said that maybe Dominee Welthagen *had* used those words. He wouldn't argue. But his point was that the Volksraad member had also said it. What was more, the Volksraad member had said it louder.

"Dominee Welthagen also declared," Gysbert van Tonder said, for the first time taking part in the conversation, "that it was an inspiration to have said nothing more about Hartman van Beek but just to have carved his name and surname on the plain foot of the rough-hewn piece of granite. Hartman van Beek's life had been like that, too – rough."

But Jurie Steyn asked if we didn't remember that the Volksraad member had said that same thing as well.

"Why, the Volksraad member said distinctly," Jurie Steyn explained, "that he was sure that Hartman van Beek would have preferred to have just that piece of undressed stone, rather than a bronze statue of him riding a horse. Or a sculptured statue of himself standing up and holding in his hand a – well, the Volksraad member didn't seem to know exactly what Hartman van Beek might be holding in his hand. A sword, likely. Or perhaps one of those long pieces of rolled-up paper with 'Traktaat' written on them. I don't know. The Volksraad member didn't say, either."

"Dominee Welthagen," Gysbert van Tonder went on, "said that Hartman van Beek would have liked that piece of raw stone better even than a sitting-down statue of himself, seeing that he was himself so unpolished. He didn't care much for brass or something else that I couldn't quite catch. I didn't care much for it myself. It sounded too foreign."

"Monumentum aere perennius," the schoolmaster pronounced. "It's Latin."

Johnny Coen observed, then, that he was pleased that what the dominee had spoken was Latin. He admitted that he had not been able to follow those words himself, exactly, either. But he had thought at the time, from the way the dominee uttered it, that it was another way of saying how ill-bred and unsmooth Hertman van Beek was, generally.

Johnny Coen said, straight out, that that was something he hadn't liked at the unveiling ceremony, the way each speaker just tried to dig up new words to say how coarse and plain-spoken Hartman van Beek had been.

"Foul-mouthed, too, I thought one of the speakers was going to say about him," Johnny Coen added, "but that speaker just seemed to stop himself in time."

He could not sincerely feel, Johnny Coen went on, that an unveiling ceremony was the right occasion to pick for calling a person names. There was a time and place for everything, he said, and if Hartman van Beek was indeed some sort of an ugly customer, they shouldn't have brought it all up *then*.

"What was more," Johnny Coen said, "every time a speaker made a particularly dirty remark about Hartman van Beek, everybody cheered. When somebody described him as an unlettered son of the soil, there was wild applause."

The conversation took a happier turn, however, when Gysbert van Tonder mentioned the horse commando that had circled the monument at sunset, Oupa Bekker riding in front.

Yes, that was something very fine, we all agreed. And what we would not forget easily, either, was the young men in Voortrekker dress firing a volley into the air as the sun was going down.

There was not the same unanimity of feeling, however, about the President Tableau, that was put on after it had got properly dark. For one thing, we had had to wait too long round that platform that had bucksails raised on it to look like a veld tent, with flaps that two Mchopis, standing one on each side of it, had to draw apart by pulling on ropes.

For another thing, we felt that they could have got some more suitable person to act the role of the President. Not that the one that took the part wasn't *good*, we said.

After all, it wasn't every day that we got somebody so prominent on the Afrikaans stage to come and present a tableau in the Groot Marico. We were honoured, of course, and we also felt that it was a great honour that was being conferred on Hartman van Beek, he being so unrefined and all. But there were some of the more conservative farmers present who felt that it would have been better if somebody else had been chosen, even if it was somebody that maybe couldn't act so well.

Then it had taken some time to get the motor-car lamps fixed in such a way as to throw a searchlight beam on the place where the opening would come in the veld tent when, at a given signal, the Mchopis pulled on the ropes.

Members of the audience had started getting impatient.

"Maak klaar, kêrels," some of them had said. "Ons moet ry."

It was already well past milking time when the car headlights were switched on and a beam of light got trained onto the platform.

Through some slight error in the manipulation of the lamps, however, the light beam missed the flaps of the veld tent and instead illuminated, very vividly, the protuberant rump of a Mchopi, who was at that moment engaged in the act of picking up a cigarette end.

Before the error was rectified there were audible, around the platform, sundry sniggers of so homespun a character that they might almost have emanated from Hartman van Beek himself.

Nevertheless, we all agreed that what followed immediately afterwards was *good*.

When the bucksails in front of the veld tent were pulled aside, there stood revealed, in the full beam of the headlights, a frock-coated figure, broad-shouldered and robust, and wearing a top hat and a presidential sash and side whiskers. In the silence that followed the frock-coated figure boomed out, in a deep voice, the well-known words of the President's last message.

Well, as we acknowledged freely afterwards, she was *good*. In this role, we said, Anna Wessels-Wessels was as good as in anything she had done since the play 'Dronk Op Haar Bruilof'. But there was something about it that wasn't just quite right, somehow. And it wasn't just because she had left a hair slide sticking out at the side of her top hat.

We were still talking about this – Gysbert van Tonder claiming that he had seen her powder puff sticking out of the upper of one boot – when young Vermaak, the schoolmaster, suddenly asked a question.

"But who is this Hartman van Beek that the monument was raised to?" he asked. "I mean . . . I mean . . . I know something about his character from what the speakers at the unveiling said. But who is he? Or who was he? Or what was he?"

We looked at the schoolmaster in surprise.

Jurie Steyn was the first to speak.

"You don't know . . .?" Jurie Steyn began. "You haven't heard . . .?"

"No," young Vermaak said bluntly, "I haven't."

Thereupon Chris Welman spoke.

"You," Chris Welman said, his tone sounding grieved. "You, a schoolmaster and all and you really don't know who Hartman van Beek was?

"But you were there – didn't you hear what all those speakers said? I mean, even if you hadn't heard of Bartman – I mean, Hartman van Beek before, you should have learnt then. And here you're supposed to be teaching children in a classroom."

The schoolmaster bridled.

"It's because I'm a schoolteacher," he said, "that I want to know what to teach my pupils. But at the unveiling ceremony not one of the speakers said anything about what Hartman van Beek *did*, to get that monument erected to him. All they talked was the usual son-of-the-veld claptrap that gets talked when any monument is raised in the Transvaal."

Jurie Steyn shook his head. Several of us followed his example. We shook our heads, also. We wanted to make it quite clear to the schoolmaster that we were shocked at his ignorance.

"But there was the horse commando," Jurie Steyn said in astonishment. "And there was that volley that the young Voortrekker men fired. You *heard* that, didn't you? Next thing you'll be saying is that there wasn't that tableau, even. Maybe you even think, now, that there *isn't* that monument there?"

This time it was the schoolmaster's turn to shake his head. He waited quite a while before he spoke.

"You know what," he said. "I don't think any of those speakers at the ceremony knew anything about Hartman van Beek, either.

"And why has that monument got only his name on it, and not the date of his birth and his death – if he is dead, that is? And that was why the Volksraad member didn't know, if they made a statue of him, what Hartman van Beek should be holding in his hand – if it is an olive branch he should be holding, or a bottle of dop. Or a pump thing for spraying cockroaches with."

Thereupon Johnny Coen said that the schoolmaster should be ashamed of himself for talking like that about a hero. It was bad enough, some of the remarks the speakers at the unveiling had passed about Hartman van Beek, Johnny Coen said.

But the schoolmaster said that was the last thing he would dream of doing. All he wanted was some information about the man we had honoured by erecting a memorial to him in our midst. And nobody seemed to know anything about him.

"I mean, who was Hartman van Beek?" the schoolmaster asked again. "Was he a leader or a statesman? Was he a missionary or a great hunter or a great fighting man? Or did he save a lot of people's lives, like Wolraad Woltemade? Or was he maybe just even a writer? What *was* he?"

We said that *that* of course, we didn't know. And did it matter, really, we asked the schoolmaster. We realised, also, that it was useless trying to argue with him.

If it wasn't enough that there were the speeches and the volleys and the horse commando *and* the tableau, then there was just nothing, we reflected, that would satisfy young Vermaak.

Rolled Gold

It was the first time young Vermaak had come to visit us in Jurie Steyn's post office since his marriage to Pauline Gerber. We could see, in several ways, the difference it had already made to the schoolmaster to be married to the daughter of a wealthy bushveld farmer like old Gerber.

For one thing, young Vermaak was now smoking expensive cigarettes out of a cigarette case made of a yellowish metal that he passed round to us so that we could help ourselves to a cigarette and at the same time see the big curved lines of his initials engraved on the lid.

We knew that the schoolmaster's initials had certainly not been by any means so important before he had married Pauline Gerber.

"If I had a cigarette case like that," Gysbert van Tonder said to young Vermaak, in handing it back to him, "I wouldn't have the letters of my Christian name and my surname cut into it so big and so fat. And so *deep*. I mean, think of how much gold gets scooped off it, that way. It's a wonder the Zeerust watchmaker that did the job didn't write his own name on it as well, and his address, so that he could prune off a whole lot more gold for himself."

Young Vermaak gazed at Gysbert van Tonder with a thin smile.

If the jeweller's graver had been set as shallow there would have been no mark at all made on the cigarette-case lid.

"It wasn't a Zeerust watchmaker," young Vermaak announced. "My monogram was engraved by a Johannesburg firm."

"I don't know whether I should not give up teaching for a while," he said. "I would like to improve my mind so that I can fit in better in the world of intellect and culture. I want to have breadth to my mind and outlook. I have been reading a book in which are described those cramping influences that fetter the spirit like a vinculum. A vinculum is the Latin word for a chain."

Gysbert van Tonder said that if that was all that was worrying the schoolmaster, then he was certainly in the right place, now, at Welgevonden, for being able to enlarge his knowlege of the world. Oom Koos Gerber, young Vermaak's father-in-law, Gysbert van Tonder said, was easily the most broad-minded man in this part of the Marico.

"I mean, just take the way Oom Koos Gerber made all his money," Gysbert van Tonder proceeded. "Well, if that's not broad-minded, then I don't know. I mean, the Bechuanas as far as Malopolole know how broad-minded Oom Koos Gerber is to this day about what brand marks there are on the cattle that he brings back to the Transvaal. That is why the Bechuanas have given him the name of RaSakèng. It means 'He-Who-Walks-Too-Near-The-Cattle-Kraal'. And if Oom Koos can teach you a few things in that line, then maybe you will get just as broad-minded. Only, I think your father-in-law will tell you that the police pay more attention today than they did in the old days to a Bechuana's complaint about missing cattle.

"So you should perhaps not start getting too broad-minded, straight away. Otherwise you'll find your wrists fastened together with a – what was that foreign word you said?"

"Vinculum," interjected At Naudé, who was quick at picking up languages.

After an interval of silence, the schoolmaster, having first self-consciously cleared his throat, proceeded to deal with the matters on which we could sense he had really come to enlighten us.

"I have booked for a number of the Grand Operas in Johannesburg," he said. "I feel that will open up a new world of culture to me. Vision is what I'll get, I think."

We could see, from the way Gysbert van Tonder opened his mouth, that Gysbert was going to ask if that was a new word for time.

"It's some of the true glory of European culture coming here to South Africa," young Vermaak went on quickly, before Gysbert van Tonder could make any more disguised reference to the penalties for cattle theft.

"And I think I'll be a better schoolteacher and more of a credit to the Education Department for having gone. You've got to wear an evening dress-suit with tails."

That was how you had to go to the Grand Opera in Johannesburg today, the schoolmaster added. And that was what gave Chris Welman, who had once worked on the mines, *his* chance to be sarcastic.

"I suppose you've also got to carry the right sort of dinner-pail," Chris Welman said, thinking of the times when he had been wont to present himself for the night shift at no. 3 shaft (and of how his colleagues would laugh at an underground man who wasn't *de règle*, but had his sandwiches wrapped in an odd piece of newspaper). "And I suppose you've also got to wear at the Opera the right kind of bicycle clips with your evening dress-suit pants."

Nevertheless – no matter what we might have pretended to the contrary – the fact was that we stood in a good deal of awe of what young Vermaak had said about the culture of Europe.

It was in recognition of this that Jurie Steyn, as though doffing his hat to the traditions of old cities, enquired of the schoolmaster, reluctantly, as to what an Opera was, exactly.

So young Vermaak got his chance to spread himself after all.

"An Opera," he said, "is a play, just like *Vertrapte Harte* or *Die Dominee se Verlossing* or *Liefde op die Ashoop*. It's like any play they have in the hall next to the flour-mill at Bekkersdal, except that it's all songs and music.

"When the warder tells the condemned man that that noise of falling bricks is the hangman's footsteps on the stairs, the warder *sings* it. And when the condemned man gets a sack pulled over his head before being hanged – like in the play *Frikkie se Laaste Ongeluk* – then the condemned man comes to the front of the stage and sings his last words.

"But what it sounds like, coming through a black sack, and all, I wouldn't know. I've just learnt about Opera from reading books about it. That is why I would like to see how it is actually done on the stage."

Gysbert van Tonder looked pleased with himself, suddenly. It seemed as though he had not been too far wrong, in having warned the schoolmaster of the dangers that lay in being too broad-minded.

"You don't only get those vinculum things on your feet, from having your ideas go too wide," Gysbert van Tonder assured young Vermaak, solemnly. "There's that sack over your head, also. It's how one thing just sort of leads to another."

The schoolmaster flared up, then. He said he hadn't come to Jurie Steyn's post office to be insulted. And here was Gysbert van Tonder talking about him as though he were already a cattle smuggler and a cattle thief – and worse. A lot worse, the schoolmaster added – thinking, no doubt, of that sack.

Thereupon At Naudé advised young Vermaak to ignore Gysbert van Tonder. *He* needn't talk, was the way At Naudé phrased it. In any case, At Naudé said, we were all eager to learn more about Opera, and if people in Operas got vinculums put on them, also, well, he was sure it was for more high-minded things than just cattle smuggling and stock theft.

But the schoolmaster said that, strangely enough, from what he had read in his book there was one Opera that *was* just like that, more or less.

The cattle part, he said, came in in the scene that was called "Exterior of the Bull-Fighting Arena". And he said that when that Opera was first produced in Paris or Munich or Rome or Sweden, or somewhere – (he forgot *where*, exactly, now, but it was some foreign place . . . Moscow, likely) – then when the curtain went up on the "Exterior of the Bull-Fighting Arena" scene, the audience all applauded when they heard a bellowing, because they expected that a real live bull would come prancing onto the stage right up to the footlights.

But the audience were very disappointed when they found that it was just the Basso-Profundo at the back of the stage practising some notes, Arpeggios, the schoolmaster called them.

"And it's queer," young Vermaak went on, "but there actually is a scene in that Opera too, that is called 'Mountain Retreat of the Smugglers'. Only, there is a beautiful girl in that

Mountain Retreat, and she is concerned only with the pleasure and the passion of the passing moment."

Well, that was something like, Chris Welman said. Several of us sat up very straight on our riempies-chairs, then, to hear more. That was something quite new to us. It looked as though those Europeans had something after all.

"She makes them aware of her charms," young Vermaak went on.

Yes, quite, we thought.

It was certainly something that had never come the way of a bushveld farmer on a cloudy night when he had cut some strand of barbed wire to let a herd of cattle into the Transvaal.

We doubted whether anything like that had ever happened even to Oom Koos Gerber himself, although everybody *knew* how lucky he was in such matters. In matters relating to cattle smuggling, that was.

"This Opera is full of colour and movement," the schoolmaster went on.

And we thought, yes, we could believe that. We could also understand young Vermaak having booked seats, then, even though it was all just music and singing.

"Then a gentle peasant girl arrives with a message for the officer who is now a smuggler," the schoolmaster proceeded.

Well, we didn't really care *what* he was – whether he was an officer or anything else – before he became a smuggler. Nor were we much interested to hear about that peasant girl, either. It was that other one that the schoolmaster couldn't tell us enough about.

"It's a very moving song that the smuggler who was once an officer sings," young Vermaak continued. "I am looking forward to hearing it. He sings it by a hole in the wall. It's through reading the message that that simple-minded girl brings him."

The schoolmaster spoke a good deal more about Opera, after that. But somehow, it never sounded quite the same again as when he first started.

Even what he said about the lovely Rhine-maiden with the lily in her hair didn't come up to the level of that other one.

All the same, as the schoolmaster went on speaking, our

attitude towards him began to change, in a singular way, with the result that we started feeling more human about him, and it seemed that there was something in what he called European culture, after all.

The result was that he afterwards set our feelings at rest with quite simple words.

"I am going to the Opera in Johannesburg with my own money," the schoolmaster said, "that I have saved up. I know I sort of tried to lie to you at the start.

"But I don't want you to think I've changed just because I've now got a rich father-in-law. I wouldn't take his money, even if –"

"Even if he offered you some," Gysbert van Tonder said, trying to sound sardonic.

Young Vermaak smiled.

"Yes," he said, "even if he offered me some – which he hasn't. And this cigarette case of mine is only rolled gold. What's more, it *was* engraved by a Zeerust watchmaker. What Joh'burg engraver can make scrolls and flourishes like that today, I mean? Here, take a look."

Coffin in the Loft

"There's nothing to be *afraid* of in a ghost," Jurie Steyn said, "so I don't know why there should be all this fuss now – people saying they won't travel by the Abjaterskop road at night."

So Gysbert van Tonder said that he had never heard of any ghost ever doing a human being harm. "Real harm, that is," he made haste to supplement his statement.

That made Chris Welman feel that he would like to go even further. There were actually instances of ghosts being helpful to human beings, Chris Welman said. Like a ghost pointing out to a party of treasure-hunters where to dig.

Ghosts were also known to have assisted in the maintenance of law and order, putting the police onto the right track when they were investigating a crime.

"Yes, and I'd like to know where the police would *be*, if it wasn't for ghosts telling them what to do," Gysbert van Tonder declared. "And not only ghosts, but a man's own neighbour, too, sometimes. A neighbour that he trusts, what's more."

So Jurie Steyn said that Gysbert van Tonder was just being silly, now. If Gysbert van Tonder thought that it was he, Jurie Steyn, that had told Sergeant Rademeyer about those long-horned cattle in the camp by the kloof, then it was the biggest mistake Gysbert van Tonder had made in his life.

"In any case, you've got nothing to complain about," Jurie Steyn ended up. "You got them out of the way in time. All except the red heifer with the white marking on the left foreleg."

"You seem to know a lot about it," Gysbert van Tonder said, sounding suspicious again. "Anyway, the markings are on the right foreleg. You can go and tell that to your friend Sergeant Rademeyer. You can also tell him that how I got the animals away in time was because I knew he was coming. I heard it from a ghost."

It took a little while, after that, for the conversation to resume a placid tenor and by that time Oupa Bekker was telling a long story about a coffin in a loft.

The ghost that stayed in that coffin was, of course, as harmless as anything, Oupa Bekker said. It would just lift up the lid at midnight and descend from the loft, using the outside stairs and not making much noise, and it would then just haunt the neighbourhood a bit, returning to its coffin well before sunrise and then letting down the lid again – and so quietly that you could hardly hear it. That ghost wouldn't hurt a fly, Oupa Bekker added.

Thereupon Johnny Coen interrupted Oupa Bekker to remark that, while we all knew that a ghost was harmless, at the same time we were none of us anxious to encounter a ghost, if we could help it.

"I mean, no matter how quiet a ghost acts, or how friendly he is, even," Johnny Coen said, "if he comes on you from behind, suddenly, and you're alone in the bush, and it's a particularly dark night, say – well, you'd rather *not* have that ghost around.

"No matter what Oupa Bekker says about how harmless such a ghost is, or about how helpful, even. I think it makes it even worse if such a ghost tries to be helpful. I don't say I'd get frightened –"

So we all said, no, of course we wouldn't get frightened, either. It wasn't a question of fear, we said. Not that we mightn't run a little, naturally, if we were on foot, or urge the horse on, slightly, if we were on horseback.

But it wasn't fear, or anything like that, we said. It just stood to reason that it was a disagreeable experience to meet a ghost alone in the veld at night. After all, it was human nature to feel like that.

Thereupon Chris Welman mentioned something he had seen just outside the Bekkersdal graveyard one night.

"It's a lonely sort of graveyard," Chris Welman explained, "and so just out of human nature I didn't worry to pick my hat up when it fell off."

Then At Naudé told us about the height of the barbed-wire fence that he had cleared at one leap near Nietverdiend, in the dark, on account of human nature and arising out of what he saw.

Before Oupa Bekker could get back to his coffin-in-the-loft story, At Naudé asked what was the strength of the report about the Abjaterskop road being haunted.

Everybody seemed to be talking about it. Not that that sort of thing made any difference to him, At Naudé said. He didn't care if the Abjaterskop road *was* haunted, seeing that he hardly ever went that way – and certainly never at night.

"Well, it seems that it was some of Gysbert van Tonder's Bechuanas who first said they saw a ghost there," Chris Welman said. "Isn't that right, Gysbert?"

"They *and* others," Gysbert van Tonder replied.

"The ghost is supposed to haunt the part of the road near the broken-down walls of the old farmhouse, that we call the murasie," Chris Welman proceeded. "That's right, hey, Gysbert?"

"That part *and* other parts," Gysbert van Tonder announced. "But mostly near the murasie."

There was something decidedly creepy in the way Gysbert van Tonder spoke, so that it came in the nature of a relief to us when Oupa Bekker returned to his coffin-ghost tale.

"What made it all seem so queer," Oupa Bekker said, "was that it was an *unused* coffin that the ghost stayed in. The coffin had been in the loft of that farmhouse for as long as almost anybody could remember."

Johnny Coen asked why they didn't go up and open the coffin and look. Oupa Bekker gazed steadily at Johnny Coen for some moments.

"Would you have liked to have gone and looked?" Oupa Bekker asked him. "In the old days, that is?"

Johnny Coen acknowledged that he wouldn't have liked it. Either in the old days or today, he said. Certainly, on his own he would not have cared to go. It would be different, perhaps, going in the company of a few people he could rely on. Say about seven or eight people.

Oupa Bekker nodded. "That's what happened in the end," Oupa Bekker said. "The farmer got a good Malay ghost-catcher up from the Cape. And when the Malay opened the coffin in the presence of the whole family, there were the mouldering bones of a human skeleton inside."

The Malay was able to tell them, also, Oupa Bekker said, that that was the kind of ghost that could never be laid. Ordinary kinds of ghosts he could catch in a bottle of sea-water that he had brought up with him for that purpose from the Cape, but the ghost in the coffin would go on haunting the place until the end of the world, becoming worse the older he got.

The police were called in, Oupa Bekker said, and they were satisfied that it was murder. A more horrible murder even than ordinary, they said, because they couldn't find any clues. And the mystery was never solved, even though the ghost gave the police what help it could.

"And the Malay was proven right," Oupa Bekker concluded. "Even after his skeleton was given decent Christian burial, the ghost kept on haunting the house. The family trekked away, afterwards, and nobody else would live in the place, which is today a ruin. That ghost is still there, and, as the Malay prophesied, with the years he gets worse."

Gysbert van Tonder yawned.

"Ah, well, I've got to be going," he said. "Maybe it would be different if I met that ghost alone in the veld at night. But on an afternoon like this – ah, well."

He walked out of the voorkamer still yawning.

"You know," Jurie Steyn said, after Gysbert van Tonder had left, "Gysbert van Tonder seemed a bit mysterious about that ghost on the Abjaterskop road, didn't he?"

We agreed that it was so.

"Well, I can see it's something he's made up – that the road is haunted," Jurie Steyn continued. "Because, from what Sergeant Rademeyer told me, that was just the trouble he had, following Gysbert and the herd of cattle, that night. It was along the Abjaterskop road, and when they came to the part near the murasie, Rademeyer's police boys said that they had heard the place was haunted, and they wouldn't go any further. That was how Gysbert van Tonder got away. Through having spread that ghost story."

After we had said, well, how's that for cunning, Jurie Steyn acquainted us with this further insight into the police sergeant's point of view:

"Well, I could, I expect, have gone on and followed him on my own," Sergeant Rademeyer had said. "I mean, I'm not afraid of ghosts. That would be absurd. But I could see it looked funny there, by that murasie, with those dark shadows amongst the trees. And the wind makes an awful sound about there, too. And I've got a wife and four children to think of. It's not that I was afraid –"

No, it was just human nature, we said, when Jurie Steyn repeated that part of the sergeant's statement to us.

But Oupa Bekker said that Gysbert van Tonder would find out his mistake, yet. And then Gysbert van Tonder would turn grey just in one night, Oupa Bekker said.

"Because the Abjaterskop road *is* haunted," Oupa Bekker said. "And by the worst kind of ghost that there is, too, now. The murasie there is the ruins of the old farmhouse with the loft. And what that ghost must be like today, I would much rather just not think."

Day of Wrath

It was what At Naudé had read in the newspapers.

Somewhere in an overseas country the people in that part had come together in a barn to wait for the end of the world, which a holy woman had gone out of her way to prophesy to them would be quite soon.

"They stopped work and sold their land for – well, I don't quite remember, now, how much they *got* for it, a morgen," At Naudé said. "But it went quite cheap. And so they just sat in the barn, waiting for the Day of Judgment."

Then Gysbert van Tonder said he wondered what those lands were like that the holy woman's followers had sold. Maybe it was just *brak* soil, and with *ganna* bushes. Well, that sort of ground you could keep, Gysbert van Tonder said. He had had experience of just that kind of lands. And what about turf soil, now, he asked – the sticky kind? There was a thing for you, too, he observed.

Thereupon Chris Welman said that if those people sitting in that overseas barn, there, wanted land so cheap that it was almost *nothing* a morgen – certainly not more than ten pounds a morgen, with two boreholes thrown in – then he himself was just the right man for them to come and talk to. Did the newspaper give the address of that barn, perhaps?

In the slight altercation that ensued between Gysbert van Tonder and Chris Welman (Gysbert van Tonder contending that he had thought of it first and that Chris Welman had no right to come and intrude, talking about ten pounds a morgen for a piece of koppie that you couldn't keep a goat alive on, not unless you fed the goat an old hat or a piece of shirt, every so often), At Naudé was able to explain, several times, that they had missed the whole point of what he was talking about. It wasn't the price of ground a morgen that the newspaper story dealt with so much as the preparations that those people were making for the Day of Judgment.

"The End of the World," At Naude stated majestically. *"Die laaste der dagen."*

He knew it would sound more solemn if he said it in Bible Nederlands instead of just in Afrikaans.

But by that time Chris Welman was saying to Gysbert van Tonder that Gysbert was pretty much like a goat himself, the way he had come butting in, and Gysbert van Tonder was saying that the way Chris Welman's trousers looked from the back, it would appear as though Chris Welman had already been feeding part of his trousers to the goats.

We felt that this was an unfortunate quarrel, between Gysbert van Tonder and Chris Welman. We sensed that it was the kind of argument that wouldn't get either of them anywhere. Moreover, when it came to a matter of dress, why, we knew that we were none of us immune from thoughtless criticism.

The jagged missiles that Gysbert van Tonder and Chris Welman were hurling at each other on the score of the respective shortcomings in their personal attire – well, a rusty old piece of that kind of weapon could wound any one of us, sitting in Jurie Steyn's voorkamer. More than one of us shifted uncomfortably on his riempies-chair, then.

But it was when Chris Welman was talking about when Gysbert van Tonder had had a haircut last that Oupa Bekker took a firm hand in the proceedings.

We were more than a little surprised that, in spite of his deafness, Oupa Bekker should have followed the argument so well. We had noticed that about Oupa Bekker before, however – that he didn't really miss much about what was going on; not when he was personally affected, that was.

"At Naudé has been talking about Judgment *Day*," Oupa Bekker said severely, at the same time moving his good velskoen forward, so as partly to hide the place in his other velskoen that was patched with a piece of rubber tubing. "And on the Day of Judgment we will none of us be judged by the *clothes* we're wearing, at the time. We'll be judged by just what we are."

From the way Oupa Bekker said it, it sounded that that would be bad enough.

So Chris Welman said that he certainly hoped, for Gysbert van Tonder's own sake, that on the Last Day Gysbert would not be judged by the kind of clothes he was wearing. If Gysbert's clothes already looked like that now, Chris Welman said, he would rather not think how they would look on the Last Day. He just couldn't imagine anything more sinful, Chris Welman added.

Before Gysbert van Tonder could think of a suitable answer, Oupa Bekker went on to say that what really was sinful was the way Chris Welman had talked of wanting to sell his ground – asking ten pounds a morgen for it – to those people in a foreign country who didn't know any better.

"Religious people," Oupa Bekker said. "Sitting there in a barn because their prophetess woman had told them that it was the End of the World. And Protestant people, too, by the sound of it."

We agreed with Oupa Bekker that they *were* Protestants, by the sound of it.

"And just because Chris Welman wants to trek to Rhodesia, as we all know," Oupa Bekker announced, finally, "he doesn't ask even if they're Catholics, first, before he thinks of selling his farm to them, which we know *isn't* worth ten pounds a morgen, just because he wants to go to Rhodesia."

Chris Welman could only say that for those people to have his farm was better than their sitting in a barn, anyway. Whereupon Gysbert van Tonder said that he wasn't so sure.

Gysbert van Tonder also said that if Chris Welman got ten pounds a morgen for his farm, then it *would* be the end of the world.

Oupa Bekker agreed with Gysbert van Tonder. Oupa Bekker said that he had known Chris Welman's farm in the old days, when it was just concession ground. And he wouldn't be sure if he didn't even *prefer* that ground like it was in the old days, before Chris Welman had made what he called improvements on it, Oupa Bekker added.

It seemed queer that Oupa Bekker should be so very much against Chris Welman. But it was only when Oupa Bekker spoke again that we understood something of the reason for it.

And we also realised in a deeper manner the truth of what we had in the course of time come to understand about Oupa Bekker's deafness: that Oupa Bekker was hardly at all deaf when there was talk going on by which he was personally affected.

"Take my own little place, now," Oupa Bekker said, "There it lies, on both sides of Papegaai Poort. *There's* a bit of ground for you, now. For somebody that wants to make a new start, and that isn't afraid of a bit of hard work. Catholic, or Protestant, *there's* now a –"

But Oupa Bekker didn't get any further. For by that time we were all laughing.

"Well, I only hope that on the Last Day I'm not found on *your* farm, Oupa Bekker," Chris Welman said. "Not when it comes to being judged, that is. And no matter what sort of clothes I had on, either. Even if I was wearing my black Nagmaal *manel*, I wouldn't fancy my chances much, if I was found walking on Judgment Day on any part of your farm. Not with all that khakibos and those erosion sloots, I wouldn't."

All the same, it was strange to think that Oupa Bekker, at his age, should also be toying with the idea of trekking to Rhodesia. Otherwise he would never want to sell his farm. It must be that Oupa Bekker had also heard about how much you could make out of tobacco, in Rhodesia. Perhaps he had also heard about how glad the Rhodesian government was to have Afrikaners trekking in there, so much so that they were asking questions about it in the Rhodesian Legislative Assembly almost every week.

It was only after At Naudé had spoken for some time again, trying to give us a clear picture of that prophetess woman and her followers waiting in the barn in their foreign country for the Last Day, that we began to understand properly what it *meant.*

And we started to think of Gabriel's Trumpet, then. And of the book in the tenth chapter of Revelations that St. John ate. And of the millions of people, the dead and the living, that would gather at the foot of Mount Zion. And of the vials of wrath. And the fall of Babylon. And the beast with seven heads.

These were things you could not reflect on just lightly.

"I wonder why they were so quick to listen to their prophet woman, the people in that foreign part," Jurie Steyn commented at length, scratching his head at the same time. "I mean, there must have been a reason, why they heeded her words and sold up so quick. After all, there was nothing that she could prophesy to them that could be half as bad as what you can read for yourself in the last few pages of the Good Book. Things like the passing of the first world in pools of fire. I have read it more than once, for myself, in a time of drought. And it has brought me a good deal of comfort, too, in a time of drought."

Well, we were in entire agreement with Jurie Steyn, there. When there had been no rain in the Marico for three years, we said, and the last water in the borehole was drying up – if you could even call it water, with all that *brak* in it – well, it was comforting, we acknowledged, to sit on one's front stoep and to read of the Day of Wrath and of the second seal being opened.

It made you feel quite happy, then, we said, to think of all the awful things that were going to happen in the world: and to think that it was all just round the corner, too, from the way the holy St. John spoke.

We were suddenly able to understand something of what must have been going on in the minds of those foreign people, who listened to their prophetess woman. Seeing that we were farmers ourselves, we understood.

"I think I see what you're getting at, Jurie," At Naudé remarked, after a while. "You get a bellyful of it, sometimes, don't you. After all, even if there isn't a drought, you do suddenly find, when you take a look over your farm, including the improvements you've made on it –"

"Especially the improvements," Chris Welman interjected bitterly, "no matter what Oupa Bekker says about them –"

"Anyway, you do get the feeling," At Naudé continued, "Revelations or no Revelations – that you've just got a bellyful."

Until that moment we had not understood, properly, why it was that there was so much solace to be found in the last twenty chapters of the Good Book, ending up with "der volken daarin brengen".

If it was the End of the World, then, at least, the End of the World would be a change. And the lure of selling up and going to Rhodesia did not have so much to do with tobacco-planting, but was a thing as old as Africa.

"It's funny, now, about Policansky," Gysbert van Tonder remarked. "But the last time I saw David Policansky, he told me he was looking for a buyer for his store. He wanted to trek out somewhere, right away from Bekkersdal, he said. And you know what – from the way that David Policansky spoke, it sounded almost as though he had also been reading the New Testament, for drawing comfort. He wasn't talking much different from what we're talking now. He would sell out quite cheap, he said, too."